Praise for Mark Frutkin

In *The Walled Garden* Mark Frutkin tend[...] he has gathered over a lifetime. Then at the end, standing back and revealing the harmonious whole, he delivers the spiritual punchline that sends us back to the first page to read again with fresh eyes.

——**Elizabeth Hay**, winner of the Giller Prize (*Late Nights on Air*)

Every one of these brief essays is itself a well-tended garden, freshly flowering wise insights. Far-flung explorations of global culture throughout the ages bolster the author's comprehensive engagement with philosophical matters, with all of the arts, especially cinema and photography, and with the origins and limitations of written language. An aphoristic style combining pith and sparkle unveils unified fields of enlightened thinking, perceiving and imagining that illumine page after page. There is much one can learn, most pleasurably, from this book.

——**Allan Briesmaster**, author of *The Long Bond* and *Windfor*

Mark Frutkin has tilled the teachings and personal epiphanies of a lifetime, and muses upon these in spartan sentences that cut to the heart of what it means to be human. Frutkin has the courage to contemplate the mysteries, including timelessness, nature as opinionless, wind and life force, etc. I couldn't put it down, walked and lived with this book, even brought it to bed with me for those darkest hours of the night when we cannot seem to see the garden that embraces us. What a gift!

——**Darlene Madott**, award-winning author of numerous books including *Stations of the Heart*, *Dying Times* and *Winners and Losers*

With this, his second collection of essays or——more accurately——*meditations*, Frutkin again turns his novelist's curiosity and poet's surprise to the simple, the arcane, the bewildering: paleolithic caves, Anne Carson's decreation, the origins of the alphabet, the importance of writing about what one *does not know*. Take welcome shelter in this garden, intimate as a love poem or a small piazza with its fountain. *The Walled Garden* reminds us that we are indeed alive and the world wondrous.

—**Nicola Vulpe**, author of numerous collections of poetry and two-time Cogswell Award winner

This book comprises meditations on a wide variety of subjects. His refusal to exhaust each topic, his tactic of suggesting what is interesting about it and then leaving the rest to the reader's imagination, accords with his characterization of any book as a "walled garden" rather than an artefact. In Frutkin's view, each book is a place of ceaseless growth and decay interacting dynamically with each reader. Elsewhere he argues that "All of reality, at least our limited view of it, is a form of fiction to begin with, based on that mutual agreement and convention." *The Walled Garden* interrogates those conventions. It is full of surprising perceptions that will force you to reassess what you think you know.

—**Susan Glickman**, author of over a dozen books in a range of genres, including essays (*Artful Flight*)

THE WALLED GARDEN

Essays on Language, Art, Film, Paleolithic Caves, Etc.

ESSENTIAL ESSAYS 83

Canada Council   Conseil des Arts
for the Arts   du Canada

ONTARIO ARTS COUNCIL
CONSEIL DES ARTS DE L'ONTARIO

an Ontario government agency
un organisme du gouvernement de l'Ont

Canadä

Guernica Editions Inc. acknowledges the support of the Canada Council
for the Arts and the Ontario Arts Council. The Ontario Arts Council
is an agency of the Government of Ontario.

We acknowledge the financial support of the Government of Canada.

THE WALLED GARDEN

Essays on Language, Art, Film,
Paleolithic Caves, Etc.

MARK FRUTKIN

GUERNICA
EDITIONS

TORONTO—CHICAGO—BUFFALO—LANCASTER (U.K.)

2023

Guernica Founder: Antonio D'Alfonso

Michael Mirolla, editor
Interior and cover design: Errol F. Richardson
Guernica Editions Inc.
287 Templemead Drive, Hamilton, ON L8W 2W4
2250 Military Road, Tonawanda, N.Y. 14150-6000 U.S.A.
www.guernicaeditions.com

Distributors:
Independent Publishers Group (IPG)
600 North Pulaski Road, Chicago IL 60624
University of Toronto Press Distribution (UTP)
5201 Dufferin Street, Toronto (ON), Canada M3H 5T8

First edition.
Printed in Canada.

Legal Deposit—Third Quarter
Library of Congress Catalog Card Number: 2023934995
Library and Archives Canada Cataloguing in Publication
Title: The walled garden : essays on language, art, film, paleolithic caves, etc. / Mark Frutkin.
Names: Frutkin, Mark, 1948- author.
Series: Essential essays series ; 83.
Description: 1st edition. | Series statement: Essential essays ; 83
Identifiers: Canadiana (print) 20230200435 | Canadiana (ebook) 20230200451 | ISBN
9781771838405 (softcover) | ISBN 9781771838412 (EPUB)
Subjects: LCGFT: Essays.
Classification: LCC PS8561.R84 W35 2023 | DDC C814/.54—dc23

CONTENTS

PROLOGUE: THE WALLED GARDEN

A book is a walled garden.

Within its covers, words sprout in tangles of leaf and root, stretching in every direction, foreseen and unforeseen. Parts of the garden are wild, other areas more domesticated, vegetables in rows, trees growing tall, other vegetation collecting underneath, some planted, others seeded by the wind.

Fruits of the most delicious and sustaining variety come to fruition here; at the same time, there may persist noxious and/or useless weeds, as well as fallen trees and dead greenery slowly rotting back into the earth. Under it all, a rich silence supports growth, ideas, thoughts and dreams.

Any book, in fact life itself, is a walled garden, with the wall of birth at one end, the wall of death at the other. No one knows what lies before or beyond.

Within the garden, nothing stays the same, all is change. Seeds sprout, branches reach and split and grow in multiple directions, vines twist upward, fruit swells, ripens, rots and falls, chaos and order intertwine, roots curl down and drive deeper and deeper into the earth.

In another sense, nothing ever changes, all is permanent and fixed, the earth supports and feeds, the sun burnishes the apple, the rain swells the grape. Silence allows the language of the book to sprout and arise. Above all, the garden, with its images of life and death, dissolution and new growth, proves to be a place of harmonious chaos.

A book, like life itself, is a walled garden.

SILENCE AGAIN: SHORT ESSAYS

1. Ox Scapulae

The earliest writing in China is found on tortoise shells or ox scapulae (shoulder blades) used for divination during the Shang Dynasty (1600-1000 BC). Inscriptions on the scapulae can be up to two hundred words long and include all the essential elements required for a Chinese writing system. The scapulae were incised with the divination question and heated in fires. The resulting cracks would then be read as the divination.

Proto-Sinaitic script in the Middle East and Egypt was developed from roughly 1800 to 1600 BC. At that time, a few hieroglyphs or images were chosen to stand in for various letters of a new phonetic writing system using an alphabet in which each letter stood for a sound. (At about the same time, the Ugaritic and Phoenician alphabets, written in cuneiform, were also being established.) Considering the use of ox scapulae by the Chinese, how odd that the first letter of the Proto-Sinaitic alphabet, the A, was represented by a hieroglyph of an ox.

What is this strange connection between the ox and written language? Oxen are castrated male cattle first domesticated around 4000 BC, probably as draft animals, and later used for ploughing. The plough, pulled by the ox, cuts lines of text in the earth.

2. Fire and Clay Tablets

In the ancient Near East, where libraries held clay tablets etched with the arrowhead shapes of cuneiform, fire would not destroy the tablets but would actually bake and preserve, or anneal, them.

In our day, we think of accidental fire primarily as an instrument of destruction, but 'to fire' something is also to harden it and ensure it lasts longer.

Further, in this context, consider that the Apocalypse for the ancient world came in the form of The Flood. In those societies, water would destroy their clay tablets (and all their records and written memory), rendering them useless. In our day, with our libraries filled with paper documents (and digital materials), the Apocalypse is most commonly imagined as arriving in the form of fire.

3. Conventional Reality

What is convention? Convention is the willing suspension of the imagination. Its addiction is spectacle. Its city is sameness, on a global scale, while its citizens are either indifferent or filled with blind, ignorant conviction. Its language is the habitual and the acceptable. Its religion is found in answers, while it fears those questions that have no answers, fears the groundless, fears boredom.

Language in this context is key. In his novel *Watt*, Samuel Beckett writes of a character: "For he could always hope, of a thing of which he had never known the name, that he would learn the name, some day, and so be *tranquillized*." (*Italics added*.) We are 'tranquillized' by conventional language, put into an unquestioning stupor and living coma by its ceaseless flow.

Convention is not evil, nor is it the enemy, it is simply a disturbing willingness to accept the false limits of the world and call that reality.

4. The Role of Empathy in Fiction

Writing fiction is all about our human ability to experience sympathy, understanding, and empathy. The old creative writing dictum, *Write what you know*, could easily prove unnecessarily limiting to the creative imagination.

Writing simply what you know could keep a writer locked into his or her own box, unable to imagine how it feels to be other. Of course, writing what you don't know can bring up a multitude of dangers. You could get it all wrong: *That's not the language used by the cancer researcher, that's not what it's like to be in prison, that's not what it's like to mine coal, that's not what it's like to be a school teacher, that's not what it's like to be an indigenous person.*

Of course, when an outsider tells the story of a group of which he or she is not a member, or even tries to become the spokesperson for that community, the anger and resentment that arises is totally justified.

Every time a writer writes about a character who is not himself or herself, or about a subject on which the author is not an expert, the writer is flirting with missing the target. However, a good writer deals in empathy and should try to get it right. How it feels to put ourselves in each others' shoes, to try to experience each others' minds and hearts, to experience empathy, which I suggest is the essence of being human – that is also the essence of fiction.

5. Now as Contradiction

We often think of the present moment as a paper-thin slice of time between past and future, something fairly easy to experience but impossible to grasp. It seems so minute and fleeting, so momentary – actually experiencing it for more than a moment becomes not only a struggle but impossible.

In fact, this moment of now isn't a paper-thin slice at all but vast and open. We can experience its vastness by relaxing into it, into its mutability, its impermanence, giving up any struggle to hold on to it – because the present is continuous, is the actual flow of future into past. It's there all the time, in every moment – omnipresent, immutable, and timeless – and never truly passes away, even though each moment appears to vanish.

FIVE-HUNDRED-WORD ESSAY

(A five-hundred-word essay on five-hundred-word essays)

During many of the early dynasties of China, scholars who wanted to advance in the world, that is, to work for the civil service, underwent rigorous, three-day exams called *juren*. The exams were held in a palace with four thousand cramped cells, complete with guards in watchtowers.

Success in the exams allowed the scholar to enter the civil service with its nine grades or levels. A position as an official brought status and numerous perks. Only scholar-officials, for example, were allowed to ride in covered carriages.

Each scholar entered his cell, which he could not leave for three days, with blank paper, ink, inkstone, and several brushes, as well as food, water, bedding, and a chamber pot. The first day's exam addressed the scholar's understanding of Confucian philosophy, including direct quotations from memory (a single error brought failure). The scholar was required to write three essays, taking three hours per essay, based on selections from writings by Confucius. Each essay, in addition to following classical rules of Chinese rhetoric, was to be no more and no less than five hundred words each. These were also known as 'eight-legged essays', with eight distinct sections.

The second day's essays, the same length, were judged on the scholar's example of advice he would provide to the Emperor based on events from Chinese history. Finally, the third day's essays, again no more and no less than five hundred words, were based on the scholar's responses to lawsuits of a sort they might judge as government officials.

The types of judgments officials would be asked to rule on could range from arguments over property, inheritance, divorce, commercial dealings, petty crimes, and more serious crimes, such as murder or enslavement.

A variety of punishments was possible. Lesser crimes could receive blows from the light or heavy rod. One could also be punished with 'registration', which meant the criminal must report to a labour unit of the army. One light-handed penalty involved the reading aloud of edifying passages from classical texts. Criminals also were given tattoos, such as the character for 'prisoner', on their faces. Capital punishment existed, including by strangulation. The most horrific punishment an official could pronounce was death by slicing.

A Song Dynasty collection by Ch'ing-ming Chi, titled *The Enlightened Judgments* (written in pale green ink), includes a dispatch that describes the four tasks of a scholar-official. The author begins with a typical Confucian statement of humility: "As a mediocre and feeble person mistakenly given a trust by an imperial order, I am anxious day and night about how I might deserve the grace of the Imperial Court and fulfill the expectations of the local literati and common people." He goes on to state the four tasks: maintain financial integrity, console the people with benevolence, be fair-minded, work diligently.

Requiring an essay of precisely five hundred words might seem like an irrelevant standard, but it would ensure brevity, concision, and attention to detail, all skills a scholar-official would later need in his daily work.

The Drawn Bow:
Reflections on Art

1. Michelangelo, the Dutch Painters and a Ming Hare

The difference between the still lifes of the master Dutch painters of the seventeenth century and the art of the Renaissance Italians (especially Michelangelo) is this: the Dutch still life of a dead hare on a plate is after the fact – the action, the vitality and the uncertainty of the hunt is long finished. In this case, the art appears to be all about technique. Though beautiful in its way, the still life, in a sense, doesn't refer to life but to art.

On the other hand, Michelangelo provides many examples of vital energy at its most intense point of expression. He focuses on the moment before the act is initiated and completed. Michelangelo's David depicts the boy standing slightly twisted, tense, ready to engage, rather than holding the already severed head of Goliath as in earlier Davids by other artists. Michelangelo's sculpture of Moses depicts the patriarch about to rise from his seat, one foot lifting from the earth.

In Michelangelo's most famous painting, on the ceiling of the Sistine Chapel, we see Adam *about* to touch the animating finger of God. Between Adam's finger and God's, there exists an electrified space, the spark of life about to overcome inherent resistance and jump across that gap, that cosmic synapse, to span the void and initiate creation. Like the Dutch masters, Michelangelo accomplishes these works with the finest application of technique. But Michelangelo also suggests something essential about life –

that the greatest intensity, the highpoint, the extreme of energy occurs a moment before action takes place. All the intention and drive has built to its maximum and is about to break through natural inertia and resistance and explode into action.

That moment is both the height of sexual tension, and the moment just before the bud sprouts from the seed and comes bursting out of its shell.

A similar expression of the same highly-energized moment is seen in a Ming Dynasty painting titled *Emperor Qianlong Hunting a Hare*. This work was painted by Giuseppe Castiglione (1688 – 1766), an Italian Jesuit brother and missionary to China, where he served as an artist at the imperial court. This painting appears to join the energy of Italian Renaissance painting with the artistic sense of China. The emperor is depicted on his horse, his bow drawn to its fullest tension, about to shoot the fleeing hare. The outcome is still in doubt. As yet, nothing has been decided or accomplished. The world remains vast and open, filled with possibility. The energy of the hunt is still on.

2. On the Monumental in Art

The American artist, Mark Rothko, once wrote: "I paint very large pictures; I realize that historically the function of painting large pictures is something very grandiose and pompous. The reason I paint them however, is precisely because I want to be intimate and human." This quote comes under the category of 'sounds good but doesn't really make sense'. Rothko doesn't explain why exactly his grandiose pictures are in fact intimate, other than his belief they are.

At the Museum of Modern Art in New York City, one can find a wall of painted cow heads by Andy Warhol. Each cow's head is exactly the same shape and size. In fact, each rectangular painting is the same cow head repeated over and over. Without passing any judgment on the ultimate worth of Andy Warhol's artistic conceptions, I will say that if this piece were not monumental, in other words if it consisted of a single painting of a cow head, it would draw little attention. The repetition leads to a kind of monumentality that attracts interest.

The monumental, or colossal, is almost *always* grandiose and pompous. You might ask, What of the Sistine Chapel? Is it grandiose and pompous because monumental? In some cases, as in this one, the context proves to be a crucial factor. The Sistine Chapel, standing alone, is certainly monumental, but the Chapel is part of a complex that includes Saint Peter's. Like the Pyramids,

Saint Peter's stands as a key symbol for the monumental, and therefore the ultimate in the grandiose and pompous. In this context, that is, in relation to the vastness of Saint Peter's, the Sistine Chapel feels rather intimate. I picture the College of Cardinals filing into the Sistine Chapel after Mass in Saint Peter's. I can't imagine they wouldn't feel that they had entered a more intimate and human space.

The monumental can also exist in the sense of an exhaustive amount of detail. On the elevated walkway called the Highline in New York City, a sculpture by Japanese artist, Yutaka Sone, is on display. The work, about ten feet by three feet, depicts the entirety of Manhattan in white marble: every building, every church, every monument, every street and park. This work is startling simply due to the monumental amount of detail involved.

In a similar vein, Geoffrey Farmer's piece, *Leaves of Grass*, displayed in the exhibit, *Shine a Light: Canadian Biennial 2014* at the National Gallery of Canada in Ottawa, is also monumental in its detail. Thousands of clippings from years of Life magazines are mounted on reeds in a display that runs for about eighty feet and can be viewed from two sides. Would this be stunning art if it weren't monumental? It is certainly impressive but would any of the clippings, or even a grouping of clippings, be of interest as art outside the context of its monumentality and monumental amount of detail?

Our society, all over the globe and through all of time it seems, has what Jonathan Jones writing in *The Guardian* called "a fever for the colossal". Jones also asked, "...does bigness make for good art?" Whether embodied in the statues of Easter Island, the sculptures of Henry Moore, Claes Oldenburg's colossal teddy bear monument planned for Central Park, the massive public art installations at Millennium Park in Chicago, or the more than a mile-long abstract earth sculpture, 'City', in Nevada by Michael Heizer, the monumental seems to capture the human imagination. But, to repeat Jones' question, 'Does bigness make for good art?'

Once, while on a train travelling from Venice to Istanbul many years ago, I noticed, as the train passed through the city of Sofia, Bulgaria, a massive painting of a communist worker holding a hammer and sickle that covered the entire side of a twenty-storey building. The best thing to be said about this example of socialist realism was that it was big. The monumental often signifies power and influence. That's why the monumental statue is so popular in fascist or totalitarian states, or even in democratic states: the oversized Lenin, the larger than life Mao, etc. Despots (and other leaders) need, apparently, to be represented on a heroic scale. Often the result enters the realm of kitsch, as in Mount Rushmore with its mountain-sized heads of famous American presidents.

Several years ago, Anish Kapoor's monumental Olympic sculpture, The Orbit, was installed at Stratford, England. Referring to the sculpture, Kapoor said, "There is a kind of medieval sense to it of reaching up to the sky, building the impossible." He added, "Like a Tower of Babel, it requires real participation from the public." But the Tower of Babel wasn't a story about public participation. It was a lesson in the dangers of humanity's hubris, the perilous longing to reach for the sky, similar to the Icarus myth but commenting on society as a whole rather than the individual.

The Wynwood Walls in Miami are another rather monumental art project. The Wynwood district near downtown Miami is filled with dozens of rundown warehouses. Someone in the city administration had the bright idea to allow graffiti artists and other artists to paint the huge walls of these warehouses with their choice of images. The art runs the gamut from amateur to cartoonish to kitsch to fantasy. Some works seem to reflect the pipe dreams of artistic druggies or to ape gang tag-art. A few of the paintings would work on paper or canvas at normal size, but not many. Nevertheless, the Wynwood Walls do prove interesting, even fascinating, for the simple fact, again, of their size and for the fact that the area exists at all. It seems highly unusual and far-seeing for a city to convert a run-down district into an outdoor art gallery. And yet, much of its interest is found in its monumentality.

The intention of the monumental in art seems to be to elicit awe from the viewer. Is the feeling of awe simply the secret ingredient that makes for great art? I don't believe so. As a viewer, I am awed by the size and scale of a work, I am awed by the amount of detail an artist might put into a piece, but I am also awed by the Grand Canyon and a summer lightning storm. Awe could be one aspect of a response to a work of art but awe, like lightning, flashes then fades.

3. The Modern Inversion of *Techne* and *Sophia*

The ancient Greeks believed that architecture, sculpture and painting represented the permanent arts (*techne*) whereas poetry, music and drama were temporary (*sophia*). Of course, this is a somewhat simplified version of complex Greek philosophical theories of types of knowledge in which 'craft', or the concrete expression of art, is contrasted with 'wisdom', or *sophia*.

One could argue that in the modern world, such a distinction between the permanent and the temporary has actually been inverted. Yes, of course, a poem, song or dramatic monologue disappears as soon as it has been spoken. But in the long view of time, most of the great classical architecture of Greece, though constructed of stone or marble, is in ruins; the sculptures are missing arms or heads; and the brilliant paintings of Greece's Golden Age of Pericles, which was an integral part of their architecture, using vivid colours on pediments and friezes, have dissolved into air and weather (not to mention being eaten away by pollution). The most lasting painted art of Greece can be found on humble pots and vases.

In the present age, the idea of the *multiple* has negated this classical distinction. How many copies of *Oedipus Rex* or *Hamlet* exist in the world today? On paper, on microfilm, tape, film, or in digital versions, in a multitude of languages? (It is estimated that *Hamlet* has been translated into 80-100 languages.) Or how many versions exist in the minds of scholars and actors, for surely someone out there has memorized the plays of the famous Greek dramatists, and I know personally of at least one actor (Raoul Bhaneja) who has the complete text of *Hamlet* in his head. These great memorizers will eventually pass on but others will take their place no doubt, and the texts will continue to survive.

Also, multiple copies of music and drama exist in many forms, as well as digitized copies of paintings, with numerous museums putting their art on line. The ancient Greek distinction between *techne* and *sophia* is no longer relevant in the age of digital technology.

STANDING STILL: NOTES ON
THE HISTORY OF PHOTOGRAPHY

1. On Standing Still

When Louis Daguerre took a photograph out his high window overlooking the Boulevard du Temple in Paris in 1839, the time required to capture the image was quite long compared to present-day photography. As a result, the only images that appear in the photo are those of things that were 'standing still': the trees along the boulevard, the buildings, the man standing in place having his boot shined. He is considered the first human being to appear in a photograph. Everyone else disappears because they are moving. No carriages or horses appear, no pedestrians, not even the boy or man shining the boots. They disappear and dissolve into their own motion and activity.

Another way of looking at this photo is from the point of view of the invisibility of labour and the labourer. The man or boy giving the shoe shine on this boulevard in Paris is invisible (in the photo) just as many of the workers in our lives are invisible – we have no idea which individual delivered the produce and meat and dairy products to our local grocery store, and we have no idea what individual grew the grapes and carrots, milked the cow or slaughtered the pig. Much of labour is like that – invisible to the consumer. We only have the product in the end. *(I have my friend, photographer Vincenzo Pietropaolo, to thank for this intriguing theory.)*

From another angle, this photograph suggests ideas about time and the relationship between photography and film. The horses, carriages and pedestrians (and the bootblack) have disappeared into their own future because they are moving through time. In a few years, they will all reappear in motion on the boulevard when the art of film (and faster shutter speeds) makes that possible.

To quote Ernest Fenollosa: "A true noun, an isolated thing, does not exist in nature." Interestingly, in *Gulliver's Travels*, Swift posits the opposite viewpoint. A certain scientist (called a 'projector') in the land of Laputa wishes to give language greater brevity by dropping all extraneous words except nouns, because, as he explains, nouns are the essence of language.

Fenollosa continues: "Things are only the terminal points, or rather the meeting points of actions, cross-sections cut through actions, *snap-shots. (Italics added.)* Neither can a pure verb, an abstract motion, be possible in nature. The eye sees noun and verb as one: things in motion, motion in things." (The flow of future becoming past.) These views seem to presage certain theories of the atom in our time – the atomic particle is neither noun nor verb, neither object nor action; not quite particle alone, not quite energy alone.

And yet, the earliest photographs could only record things standing still, that moment between actions, that moment when both noun and verb have come to a momentary stop. Or perhaps better to say, that moment when the verb is swallowed in the noun, as the light has been swallowed in Daguerre's camera.

2. Notes on Photography

Why do so many of the great inventions arise from different inventors at the same time? This is clearly true of photography, as well as radio. For photography, 1839 was the year. Niepce, Daguerre, Fox Talbot, Herschel, Bayard, Hercules Florence (in the interior of Brazil) and others in Poland, France, Germany and Scotland were all announcing their sometimes quite divergent photographic techniques all in the singular year of 1839. Of course, the ground had been prepared by many previous technical developments but 1839 seemed to be the year of photography's first technical fruition.

***

The titles of many of the early photographs begin with the words: View from a window – at St.-Loup-de-Varennes, at Lacock Abbey, and many others. Even though Daguerre did not include the words 'view from a window' in the title, his famous photo, Boulevard du Temple, was certainly taken from a window.

***

In all the early portrait photographs, no one smiles. When, I wonder, did the first smile appear in a photo? And why? What changed to make a person want to smile in a photo or to make a photographer want to suggest it. Now, and throughout my lifetime, it has been so ubiquitous as to be almost invisible – 'Smile!'

Several theories present themselves. Bad teeth and the need to keep them hidden? Or the long exposure times required for early photographs? Holding a smile too long feels forced and unnatural. But by the early 1840s, exposure times had already been reduced to ten seconds. The first smile in a photo – when was it taken and where is it now?

***

What film delivers that photography cannot is time, duration. What photography can provide, that film seldom does (except for a few filmmakers, such as Tarkovsky) is the contemplative moment, an instant cut off from the flow, or perhaps, a particle of the flow, a pause, a slice of time, utterly alive in its stillness.

TIMELESS

Adam Gopnik, in his book of essays titled *Winter*, calls the cold season 'a timeless world', and adds "We share a sense of a timeless winter, of eternal winter, of winter as the place where time stands still …"

Winter in Canada can certainly feel 'timeless' or perhaps we should say 'endless'. However, I believe the summer season provides a stronger sense of timelessness, with its boundless idylls where the weekends bleed into the week, and one month is indistinguishable from the other. The period from Canada Day to Labour Day (for some) is a sun-filled void of lying on the beach or on a chaise, book in hand, evenings lasting until 9:30 or later, and limitless time spent outdoors under open, undefined sky.

Perhaps childhood, with its unstructured summers between school years, is the ultimate source of this feeling but it certainly lingers into adulthood with its extended summer holidays and long weekends.

In much of Canada in particular, the workaday world, with its clocks and calendars, is a winter world, a world of dusk descending by 3:30 or 4:00, a world of artificial light. For me, the winter world is a world of time, whereas summer days are indistinguishable one from the other. It hardly matters if this is Monday or Friday, if no labour calls for attention.

CLOCKS AND BELLS

When the world of Christendom switched from using church bells as the means to mark time to keeping time with clocks, everything changed. The sacred and the secular were separated. Time became more precise, more scientific. Time was something that was manufactured, the product of a machine.

Because time was no longer a facet of the everyday linked to religion, the traditional religious impulse has clearly begun to ebb ever since, never mind the fundamentalist desperation to hold back the inevitable tide. Now, when I hear church bells, the main feeling inspired is one of nostalgia, pleasant enough in its own way but somewhat de-linked and detached from both the business of life and its genuine spiritual aspects.

ANNE CARSON AND *DECREATION*

1.)

In her book titled *Decreation* (Vintage Canada, 2005), Anne Carson, one of today's most intriguing writers and poets, defines the word 'decreation' as a kind of melding with God through an 'undoing of self'. She explores the term by visiting the lives of three extraordinary women: Sappho, the ancient Greek poet; Marguerite Porete, burned at the stake in Paris in 1310 for refusing to recant her heretical views on Divine Love; and Simone Weil, the twentieth-century French philosopher. In each case, the ultimate union is one of the disappearance or dissolution of the self into a divine ecstasy.

I find an intriguing connection between decreation and a Buddhist view of egolessness. Egolessness is the non-theistic version of decreation. In both cases, the self dissolves. In the theistic view, the self dissolves into the Godhead, although the descriptions of the experience of these three women seem hardly separable from the experience of egolessness. With egolessness (and let me be clear, I am talking from an intellectual level here, not from an experiential one), the self dissolves into vastness, brilliance, a timeless space and light. In other words, the self releases back into that linked dyad of great abstractions – eternity and infinity. Some might call this God. Some might call it what it is. In any case, any intellectual, word-bound description of the experience is limited. Not the moon itself but the finger pointing at the moon.

Carson suggests that the dissolution of self is tantamount to experiencing the ecstasy of divine love. Perhaps that is why the act of sexual union in its most extreme ecstasy contains a sense of dissolution. In the sexual act, there persists a deep human hunger and longing to dissolve the self into the other. That is one reason it is so satisfying and addictive – we want a taste of the ultimate, to let go of our burden of selfhood, for a moment at least.

2.)

In *Decreation*, which includes poetry, essays, and opera, Carson also appears to bring together certain elements from Christian mysticism and Vajrayana Buddhism.

When Carson explores the concept of the 'annihilated' self of the mystic, Marguerite Porete, she ultimately delivers us into the space of brilliant emptiness that is the key hallmark of esoteric Buddhism.

In the voice of Porete, Carson writes, "Love erases the world and time". Later, in The Aria of the Flames, she imagines Porete singing from her burning pyre: "Where else can God put God's emptiness, where else can God put God's nothingness, where else can God put God's endless end, but in me? … Where else can God put God?"

If the self of Marguerite Porete has been annihilated by its pouring itself completely, wholly, and utterly into love, and if God can only mirror itself in that annihilated self then God too has been annihilated, and is the essence of emptiness and its brilliance.

NATURE HAS NO OPINION

Whether the fire burns a porn mag or a Bible, nature has no opinion. Whether the hurricane flattens an orphanage or a prison, nature has no opinion. Whether the flood drowns innocent dogs and cats or an evil tyrant, nature has no opinion. Whether the earthquake destroys a cluster-bomb factory or a sacred church or temple, nature has no opinion.

WIND AND LIFE FORCE

Wind is perhaps the most perfect metaphor for life force. Both are invisible. Life force literally moves the world, but, like the wind, it is only visible in its effects. The gesture of a hand, raising the eyes to the heavens, the next breath are all prompted and driven by life force but life force is invisible.

The fan-shaped leaves on the gingko tree flicker in the wind but we don't see the wind. The clouds sail past, our sweating forehead is cooled, the child's hair is ruffled, all driven by the invisible wind, which is seen only in its effects.

ON MAGIC REALISM

British author, Geoff Dyer, in *Jeff in Venice, Death in Varanasi*, writes: "After a fling with Gabriel Garcia Marquez, I'd come to detest even a hint of magic realism in fiction. As soon as I come to a passage in a novel where the trees started talking to each other, I gave up on the spot."

Nevertheless, later in the same book, I am surprised to read that Dyer has a conversation with a talking goat that goes on for several pages. I'm not sure a talking goat is any better than talking trees, but I suppose his justification would be that he was on drugs at the time.

In one sense, we are all on a drug all the time – the drug of mutual agreement as to the terms and limits of reality. All of reality, at least our limited view of it, is a form of fiction to begin with, based on that mutual agreement and convention. Magic realism can be a glimpse behind that veil.

PALEOLITHIC CAVES

1. Paleolithic Cave Art Theories

Archeologists and cave experts have been attempting for well over a century to find a single, overarching impetus for the art found in Paleolithic caves. Over the years, some have claimed that all or most cave art was primarily connected to descriptions of the hunt, or that it was a form of sympathetic magic to help ensure a successful hunt in the future. The problem with this theory is that the bones of animals found in most caves are not from the animals depicted on the walls. In most cases, the cave dwellers weren't actually eating what they were drawing, which seems to discount any overriding connection to the hunt, through sympathetic magic or otherwise.

Others have claimed that the cave paintings are primarily a shamanistic endeavour and have shown numerous images as proof, or have compared present-day aboriginal and indigenous understanding and practices of shamanism with the images. Or they have stated that the paintings are part of early man's death rituals. Or that the works are part of tribal or clan expressions and totems. Still others have claimed the cave paintings (and sculptures) are simply art for art's sake. A more recent claim states that the caves are a great, unified theory of creation. All of these theories could be partially true but it seems clear that no single, unifying theory of any kind exists to explain the cave paintings.

Let us look at the past three thousand years or so and explore the wide variety of reasons people around the world in all cultures have produced art since the time of the Egyptians. These include religion, mysticism and shamanism, politics, personal status (portraits), commerce (to sell or market something), to promote one's side in war, and simply art for art's sake, and so on.

Stylistically, this history of art includes realism, perspective, two-dimensional art, abstraction, conceptual art, performance art, land art, and everything in between and beyond. If you expand the idea of art to include images of any kind, we could add street signs, billboards, films, photographs, and the hand that signals 'stop' to pedestrians before they cross the street. Why include images of all kinds such as street signs? Because the caves too include images of all sorts, the hand being a popular one found in many caves (resembling to a striking degree those hands at crosswalks). The cave paintings also often include dots, circles, lines, apparently random signs, and other abstractions as well.

The cave paintings, at least the ones we have found thus far, were executed over an incredible stretch of time, perhaps as much as thirty thousand years. Compare this to our rather paltry historical time period of roughly four thousand years. Recent discoveries have shown that some caves include art works that were done five or ten thousand years after the original works in the same cave, with later artists adding their own work to work already there.

It hardly seems credible that any single theory could explain all the cave paintings, or even the majority. How could one artist, after a passage of five or ten thousand years, possibly know the views and beliefs of earlier artists – this without any recourse to written language? It staggers the imagination. We, with all our science and ability to record images and words, barely know anything definitive about pre-history, other than what we can gain from archeology. We certainly know little about the reasoning of the people who painted the caves. It's almost all guesswork. So how could the second or third or tenth wave of cave artists know anything of the earlier artists and their beliefs? All the later artist really had to work from was the earlier art itself (just like us), and possibly through some sense of oral history.

Still, there exist strange anomalies in Paleolithic cave art that will always raise questions. The caves contain no drawings or paintings of landscapes, no suns or moons, no stars, little plant life, almost no birds, few fish. The paintings in caves are overwhelmingly of mammals.

In the end, we cannot help but see ourselves in remote cultures and distant times. We are always looking into a mirror and perceiving ourselves at another time. We will probably do the same when we meet aliens from outer space. We certainly do it when regarding Paleolithic cave art. But to do so is irresistible – this is our deep past, ourselves at the dawn of culture. Without a doubt, we will continue questioning and searching to try to find out who we are.

2. Paleolithic Cave Art and Picasso

Consider a photograph of Picasso in which he stands by the sea with a horned bull's mask on his head. Of course, Picasso loved the world of the bullfight but the photo also suggests connections to Paleolithic cave art as many ancient paintings in the caves of France and Spain represent horned mammals such as bulls, bison, and aurochs.

Picasso's *Vollard Suite*, a collection of one hundred of the artist's etchings made between 1930 and 1937, includes numerous images of bulls, the Minotaur, horses, as well as a number of nude women. Many of these reveal Picasso's incredible ability to etch figures and scenes with a minimal use of line. But, besides the obvious connections to the cave paintings in terms of subject matter (bulls, etc.), a percentage of the works in the *Vollard Suite* also include images that are superimposed, flurries of energized lines that are highly reminiscent of paintings in some of the caves such as Lascaux (especially on the North Wall of an area called the Apse), on the walls of the Inner Gallery at Comberelles, and at Les Trois Frères cave (in an area called the Sanctuary). Examples from the *Vollard Suite* that echo these superimposed cave paintings include the following images: #3 (At the Bath), #6 (Nude Woman in Front of a Statue), #16 (Death in the Sun, IV), #22 (Female Bull Fighter, II), #76 (Sculpture and Vase of Flowers), #88 (Wounded Minotaur, VI); and especially #18 (Heads and Figures Entangled). Although some critics claim that Paleolithic art had a minimal influence on Picasso, the similarities are difficult to ignore.

The timing too is relevant. Picasso did most of his work in the first half of the twentieth century when many caves were being discovered and explored. It's not beyond belief that he could have literally walked from his studio in southern France to one of the local painted caves. Those discovered earlier, in the nineteenth century, were also being re-studied and re-evaluated. It's hard to believe that Picasso was not influenced by the Paleolithic paintings, particularly when one considers his work itself (especially the *Vollard Suite*) with its powerful echoes in terms of style and subject matter of the art found in the caves.

INVISIBLE SOCIETIES

In the past two hundred years, the invisible material world was revealed by science through such discoveries as electromagnetic waves, x-rays, bacteria, viruses, atoms, and quanta. At the same time, Freud, Jung, and others were uncovering the invisible psychic and dream worlds of the individual.

In our own era, we are now discovering the existence of invisible societies. Of course, the nation state is still the prevailing social and political structure. But the Internet, in particular, has made it possible to form numerous other more or less invisible societies. Social and political groups, of all stripes, are forming outside the parameters of the nation state and normal structures of society. When I sign a petition from Avaaz or any number of other online groups, or donate to those groups, I'm part of an invisible society made up of individuals that I have never met and likely never will meet. This group could be national, multi-national, or global. In terms of my views of the environment, society, and politics, I might have more in common with an Italian, a Japanese, or a Peruvian citizen than with a neighbour down the street.

Society is revealing its invisible aspect in other realms as well. I can play chess on the Internet with people I've never met or I can be involved in online gaming with a host of other players. These social groups are made up of people who are invisible to each other. I can become the member of an invisible society of shoppers by purchasing something on Amazon, eBay, or from a drugstore in Winnipeg that I've never entered. Despite never having met, we have a connection. We form an invisible society.

Time and Eternity

Just as Time is sculpted out of Eternity, order is constructed out of infinite chaos. In that sense, Time is actually made of Eternity; and order – our workable, understandable world – is also made out of the primordial chaos. We don't have to see chaos as Dionysian, or the dark side, because it is the same stuff that forms order.

Even as a statue of marble falls over in the jungle and is worn away over vast time, turning back into simple faceless stone, so does Time come to an end, dissolving back into its greater self, Eternity.

As the trees and plants are expressions of earth, they will ultimately return to that earth whence they came. All this world is nothing more than sparks of light reflecting from the mirror of emptiness; words, poems, songs arise from silence and fall back into silence, breath tasting the air and giving back into air, rain falling in a river.

THE BOOK DISAPPEARS

Like something out of a story by Jorge Luis Borges, some years ago an Argentinian publisher produced a book – an anthology of new Latin American fiction – printed with ink that disappears, fading away within two months after the book's plastic packaging is removed. What a fabulous, and disturbing, metaphor for the fading of the book in our time, as well as how quickly readers lose interest and move on to the next novelty.

Orange Gardens and Bedsprings: A Theory of Language

The moon bird's head is filled with nothing but thoughts of the moon
—**Kabir**

In some of the finest, most intriguing writing, the form and structure of the words and lines echo their content. Today, we find Wordsworth's long line depicting the long lake a touch obvious:

> the slopes
> And heights meanwhile were slowly overspread
> With darkness, and before a rippling breeze
> The long lake lengthened out its hoary line …

The final line, in particular, is structured by the poet to reflect the content. I believe a more subtle approach can be found in the following examples, two from Samuel Beckett, one from Joseph Conrad, and several from other sources. These selections explore the possibilities of what can be done with language when the form perfectly echoes the content, when what is said is replicated and reinforced in how it is said.

In Chapter Nine of *Murphy*, Beckett's first novel (1938), Ticklepenny, the caretaker at an asylum, is showing Murphy a tiny garret where he will be living while employed by the institution. In the room, Murphy spots a sagging bed of which Beckett writes: "The bed, *so low and gone in the springs that even unfreighted the middle grazed the ground*, was wedged lengthways into the cleft of floor and ceiling, so that Murphy was saved the trouble of moving it into that position." *(Italics added.)*

The italicized phrase reflects the look of the bed, with the unusual heavy word, *unfreighted*, in the middle, dragging down the phrase even as the centre of the bed sags toward the floor. Beckett could have written 'empty' instead of 'unfreighted', but he chose a heavier, and rather unusual, word precisely appropriate to the context.

On the next page in the same novel, Beckett showcases another masterful example of this type. Murphy is worried about getting heat up to the garret. Since a brazier is forbidden, Murphy suggests that a heating device be attached by 'tubes and wires' (essentially, what we would call 'extenders', that fit into one another like extension cords) to heat sources he has seen earlier on lower levels. Ticklepenny hesitates – he explains that no tubes and wires at present reach the "remote aery".

Beckett writes: "He (Murphy) went on to speak of tubes and wires. Was it not just the beauty of tubes and wires, that they could be extended? Was it not their chief characteristic, the ease with which they could be extended? What was the point of going in for tubes and wires at all, if you did not extend them without compunction whenever necessary? Did they not cry out for extension? Ticklepenny thought he would never stop, saying feverishly the same thing in slightly different ways."

On first reading this paragraph, I did not see the reflection of "tubes and wires" in the series of short lines, similar to each other, of varying lengths. On rereading however, I noticed that Beckett tells us that he knows exactly what he is doing by adding the last line: "...saying feverishly the same thing in slightly different ways." The different lengths of line and the repetitions of the words 'tubes and wires' and 'extend' perfectly replicate, in language, the appearance in reality of various extension cords or tubes, similar but different, which could be linked together to reach the remote attic from lower levels, just as the short phrases and sentences are linked together to form a paragraph.

Joseph Conrad, in his novel, *Nostromo* (1904), has provided a similar example of form echoing content on a broader scale. Chapter One opens with the following description in its *first* sentence, "In the time of Spanish rule, and for many years afterwards, the town of Sulaco—the luxuriant beauty of the orange gardens bears witness to its antiquity—had never been commercially anything more important than a coasting port with a fairly large local trade in ox-hides and indigo."

Eight pages later, in the *final* sentence of Chapter One, Conrad completes his description of the town, "The town of Sulaco itself—tops of walls, a great cupola, gleams of white miradors in a vast grove of orange trees—lies between the mountains and the plain, at some little distance from its harbour and out of the direct line of sight from the sea."

What first caught my eye was the construction of the sentences, each with an appositional phrase set off by dashes. This sentence structure (a phrase set off by dashes) appears nowhere else in the chapter. Thus, the entire chapter (and the two phrases themselves) are contained, or blocked off, in the same way the orange gardens are confined and restricted in walled gardens, between the 'walls' of the dashes. This too reflects the town of Sulaco itself, caught between mountains and plain. It is even out of sight of the sea, as walled gardens are "out of sight".

Furthermore, I might even argue that the opening phrase, "In the time of Spanish rule, and for many years afterwards", followed by the reference to "antiquity" accomplishes the same blocking construction with Time itself.

I have come across similar examples in several other works as well. Canadian poet Don McKay pulls it off in some of his best poems. For example, in the prose poem, 'Waking At the Mouth of the Willow River' from the collection titled *Night Field* (1991), he begins, "Sleep, my favourite flannel shirt, wears thin, and shreds, and birdsong happens in the holes" wherein the pauses occasioned by the commas replicate the holes in the flannel shirt.

In the Introduction to *A Journey Through the Aegean Islands* (1988) by George Galt, the author writes: "Up this way, up that, I climbed the winding streets of Naxos town one May morning...," in which the author simply and perfectly echoes the switchback aspect of a steep grade in a Greek village.

Another example, this from Patrick O'Brian's sixth volume in the Aubry-Maturin series, *The Fortune of War* (p. 281), depicts a hen announcing the arrival of an egg she has laid on board the deck of an English warship: "The proud cock crowed, clapping his wings in the first rays of the sun, and a hen cried out that she had laid an egg, an egg, an egg!" The triadic repetition of 'an egg' perfectly echoes the three cries of the hen.

The question of the author's intention certainly arises in some of these cases. Were these examples in any way unintentional? Perhaps, but I doubt it.

In my own case, there have been times when I began writing a sentence and realized halfway through that I could adjust the sentence or paragraph to a form that reflected and resonated with the content. I believe this style is seldom predetermined but comes about through immersion in the act, in the midst of writing. The unintentional dissolving and resolving into the intentional. That is the way it arose for me in the following examples from my own work, particularly in the travel volume, *Walking Backwards*, and in the novel, *Fabrizio's Return*.

In *Walking Backwards*, the chapter titled 'Boulder, Colorado, 1976', concludes with a journey in which my friend David and I hitchhike across the American plains: "Later that day, after receiving a number of rides, we stand in the middle of Kansas surrounded by hundreds of miles of cornfields, the wind whipping steadily with nothing to stop it in any direction, not a tree not a building not a hedge just a thousand miles of tall green corn stalks and wheat waving in the stiff wind that pumps steadily without pause without cease without a break across three flat states all of which look like perfect rectangles on the map, while next to me as I stand by the highway with my thumb in the air, David is once again doing tai chi looking like a disjointed flamingo or a pine tree trying to take flight in this steady Kansas wind."

The long fluid sentence, with little punctuation, is, of course, meant to reflect the way the wind flows steadily across the flat, open landscape with nothing to impede it.

Another example from the same book is found in the chapter on the city of Venice: "The quiet courtyard next to the San Giorgio dei Greci Church—it is completely separated from the world by its high wall—contains the following: a typical Venetian capped well circled at its foot by three levels of steps, a few towering trees, a marble bench and a lofty campanile with an obvious tilt."

In this case, the separation of the courtyard from the city is represented by the phrase set within dashes. In fact, the reference to the separation itself appears within said dashes.

A final example is found in my novel, *Fabrizio's Return*:
"Ugo the Mantuan, thick-lipped, hunch-backed, his mastiff at his side, trudged the rooms of his vast and exfoliating palace. Each time he came to a room where he had previously seen a doorway leading out, he was discouraged to find that his longed-for exit had vanished and in its place had appeared another set of seven, eleven, or possibly even thirteen rooms he did not recognize and which must have been constructed since his dream had begun numberless years before. He noticed that his thoughts, too, reflected the complexity of the maze for he could not form a decent, simple, perfectly understandable sentence in his own head because the words were constructed of fear and sadness and they wouldn't join together like good bricks for building but kept being interrupted and crossed over by other sentences which began in the middle and continued on and on and never seemed to come to an end, or at least an exit, a waking from this lost wandering in a palace without limit and without egress."

In this case, similarly, the endless, exit-less palace and the thoughts of Ugo are reflected in the complexity and the run-on pattern of language used.

*

On another level, an extraordinary and subtle example of the form echoing content device is found in the ancient Taoist parable, The Allegory of the Stray Sheep, which the translator Jean Levi calls "a kind of anti-fable". Meant to depict the Taoist view of how the

'One' becomes the 'Many', the story relates how a large group of villagers (we humans) joined together to search for a single lost sheep (the Way). Because the landscape offered a multiplicity of forking paths, numerous people were required for the search. The student who was asked to explain this parable told another parable as explanation, and the teacher, when asked to explain this second parable told still another parable, all of which were rather obscure and difficult to understand. The parables themselves kept forking off in different directions like the paths. The stray sheep was never found, of course.

According to fundamental Taoist teaching, the Way cannot be explained or expressed. The forking, telescoping parables reflect the way the paths diverge and split and, furthermore, show what happens to any attempt to fix an ultimate explanation of the Way in words. Actually putting your hands on the sheep would bring everything to an end.

*

And finally, perhaps the ultimate, most transcendent version of this device is found in the Heart Sutra, a root text of all Buddhist traditions. The Heart Sutra, like the Old and New Testaments, is not only a religious text but a literary one as well. Literary, philosophical and psychological. The set-up for The Heart Sutra is almost theatrical: the three characters include Sariputra, the student who asks the question and puts everything in motion; Avelokiteshvara, the teacher who will attempt to explain ultimate wisdom; and the Buddha himself who says nothing until near the end but whose silent presence supercharges the atmosphere.

The Heart Sutra is said to be a teaching on Emptiness but this is not emptiness in any way the word can be defined in English. Avelokiteshvara explains that ultimate wisdom is not found in form or non-form, it is not found in suffering or non-suffering, or in any of the other dualities that make up our language and limit our understanding. So, the ultimate is not found in words nor is it found in silence. Those are simply reflections of each other – take the image away from the mirror and nothing appears in the mirror. Meanwhile, the Buddha stands by in silence, showing by his mere presence what ultimate wisdom looks and feels like.

In the end, wisdom is not in words, and not in silence – and yet, Sariputra needs to ask the question or nothing happens, Avelokiteshvara needs to try to answer the question, and the Buddha's presence is required for the revelation to happen, so Sariputra can understand, and glimpse the truth. We need the words, but the words aren't it. We need the silence, but the silence isn't it. It seems to suggest that all of this is the mist of a dream, all this reaching and all this seeking. The reason wisdom is not in the words and not in the silence is because it is already present, has always been present, will always be present. The Buddha simply embodies it and says, without saying it, it's already here, wake up to it.

The Buddha's state of mind itself reflects perfectly what the words of the sutra are trying to say. The wisdom of form reflecting content.

ZERO

In Amir D. Aczel's bestselling book, *Finding Zero*, about his hunt in the Far East for the origins of the number (or non-number) zero in our distant mathematical history, he refers numerous times to the Buddhist concept, *shunyata*, which he and others he consults define as emptiness, or nothingness, or the void. He and others see *shunyata* as the philosophical source for zero.

While a Buddhist philosophical view would certainly define *shunyata* as emptiness, it is hardly the equivalent of what we in the West mean by that term. There is nothing nihilistic in the term *shunyata*, whereas the word 'emptiness', for a Westerner, is the essence of nihilism.

Shunyata is perhaps more correctly defined as openness, which can be seen as empty, but is actually filled with possibility, with the energy and light of the creative. If there were no open space, no emptiness, nothing at all could arise, nothing could begin, nothing could exist.

Without the open space of emptiness, of *shunyata*, charged and filled with radiance and possibility, the world and everything in it could not possibly exist.

Nature Has No Opinion (Again)

When I write 'nature has no opinion', is that the same as film director Werner Herzog's view of nature as being 'overwhelmingly indifferent'? I don't believe so – Herzog's view is laden with and limited by human emotion. 'Nature has no opinion' is larger than that, more vast.

'Overwhelmingly indifferent' is a comment that clearly reveals its emotional content. It claims that nature doesn't care about me personally, or any of us. This emotive response to nature weighs one down.

'Nature has no opinion' is more Zen-like, lighter, less emotive. It simply states the view that there are things out there larger and/or deeper than us and our opinions, and there is no reason to consider that fact a cause for depression or angst. In fact, it's liberating.

WIT AND FAMILIES

Just because a saying is witty or has a rare literary pedigree doesn't mean it is true. Tolstoy wrote in the first line of *Anna Karenina*, "Happy families are all alike; every unhappy family is unhappy in its own way." This has the momentary ring of truth and certainly stands as a fine way to begin a novel.

However, it's clearly untrue. On closer inspection, there is no such thing as a 'happy' or an 'unhappy' family. All families exist on a continuum, a complex range of happiness and unhappiness (whatever those words mean).

But, of course, that's why fiction is different than sociology.

Short Essays on Film

1. The Question and the Message in the film *Arrival*

In the film *Arrival*, the aliens have arrived on earth but the film is much more than a sci-fi thriller or a science and tech orgy, like so many recent films on the same or similar subject.

Quebec director, Denis Villeneuve, uses the character Louise Banks, a linguistics professor played by Amy Adams, to pose an intriguing question: If you saw what would happen in your entire life, past and future, would you change anything? In the context of the film, Adams sees a future in which her baby daughter will grow up and, as a young woman, die of a rare disease, which might be some form of cancer. Of course, she doesn't choose that her child not be born at all. Clearly, she realizes that the joys of life include the other side which we recognize as pain and suffering.

But it's an absurd, impossible question. We can't change anything about our lives. We certainly cannot go back into the past and alter events that have already happened. And, as for the future, we might think we have the free will to choose what direction things might take but we are fated to make those choices that free will allows. In other words, fate and free will are the same. This is not quite the same as saying that free will is an illusion, for we are free to make choices but how we act on that freedom is fated. (Some might call this karma, but that's another subject.) To realize that they are the same is to answer the question, 'No, I wouldn't change anything in my life, past or future. I *can't* change anything and

I *choose* not to change anything.' The image that arises for me is that, at the moment of death, we enter the mirror and realize that that moment is the perfect moment to die, that is the moment that, somehow, we choose.

All of which brings us to the question of Time. In the film, Adams is attempting to communicate with the aliens but nothing clicks until she realizes their language isn't linear and temporal like ours. We go from one word to the next and the end of this sentence is in the future until it arrives. And then it's in the past. And that relationship with language affects and determines how we think about Time and Reality. However, the aliens have a different view of language, and a different relationship with Time. Their language, like their sense of Time, is circular and feels holistic, not linear.

Past and future exist in the present. Let's examine that. The present is nothing more than the *process* of the future becoming the past. The past no longer exists, the future does not yet exist. But, the truly shocking thing is that there is no fixed moment called the present, there is only this process of future becoming past. Nothing to fixate on, nothing to hold onto. And yet, this process is always happening, future in every moment is becoming past. That shooting star never stops, never burns out. Because it isn't fixed in a distinct, isolate moment, the present is both empty and eternal.

2. Tarkovsky and Milk

In Russian director Andrei Tarkovsky's film, *Stalker* (1979), he shoots a domestic scene that takes place in the kitchen of the main character (named Stalker) and his wife. The couple have been arguing about his plans to leave temporarily their domestic situation and their child to go off to explore the mysterious 'Zone'. On the kitchen table stands a full glass of milk that somehow is knocked over during their argument. Tarkovsky spends a lot of film time watching the flood of white as it expands, covering the table and dripping to the floor. The spilling of milk here, I believe represents a break in the warmth and bond of their familial relationship.

Scenes of spilt or splattered milk also appear in the films *Andre Roublev*, *Mirror* and *Nostalghia*, as well as in Tarkovsky's later, and last, film, *The Sacrifice*.

In *The Sacrifice* (1986), a well-off extended family has come to their country house on an island in Scandinavia to celebrate the sixty-fifth birthday of the paterfamilias. While the family and the maids are momentarily absent from the scene, the camera explores the spacious dining room of the house. Against the wall stands a tall sideboard with shelves. Near its top shelf rests a capacious glass milk jug. As the camera scans this domestic scene, unexpectedly the silence is fractured by what sounds like a pair of jets flying low over the island and the house. As the jets approach, the entire house begins to shake, the tall sideboard with it. As the jets are heard passing overhead, in a scene that is one of the great images of twentieth century filmmaking, the jug teeters and falls to the floor where it shatters, the explosion of milk covering the wooden floor.

Soon after, the family hears on a radio broadcast that something extremely disturbing and cataclysmic is about to happen in the outside world: all-out war and possibly nuclear holocaust. Looking back, the viewer can see that the scene ending in that white milky blank is suggestive of the finality of a nuclear explosion. How fascinating that Tarkovsky uses milk for this scene, milk being a symbol of nurturing and fertility, domesticity and life. This is a perfect contrast to the idea of nuclear annihilation which is diametrically opposed to that sense of tender vitality.

3. Notes on Tarkovsky's *Andrei Rublev*

Andrei Tarkovsky's film, *Andrei Rublev* (1968), set in medieval Russia of the 1400s, tells the story of a famous icon painter while subtly addressing the role of the artist in society. The prologue of the film depicts a man being chased by a mob in half a dozen boats. He lands his own boat, runs up a hill, climbs the tower of a church and, bizarrely, harnesses himself into a rudimentary hot air balloon that looks as if it has been assembled out of large leather bladders. He then takes off, hanging under the balloon, and escapes. He is thrilled and excited to be floating above the landscape but soon comes crashing down to his death. This Icarus figure (the fact that he uses a balloon and not wings is absurdly humorous) has no narrative connection to the rest of the film but sets the theme – the artist might take flight and escape the mundane world at times but, in the end, he and his works will always be brought down to earth. But, as Tarkovsky mentions elsewhere, "art would be useless if the world were perfect," adding that for the artist to venture forth is more important than ultimate success or failure. As Canadian poet Don McKay writes in his poem, 'Icarus': "Icarus isn't sorry." Icarus fails in the end but the artist must make the attempt to fly.

***

Scenes in The Bell section of the film, in which a multitude of characters are constructing a huge bell for a church, are reminiscent of certain paintings by the Breugels, Elder and Younger – distant views of landscapes crawling with workers, priests, animals, and nobility on splendid horses.

***

An earlier chapter of the film shows a small group of people (seven or eight) in the medium distance in an empty church. They are depicted at various distances from the viewer, all facing the camera. The tableaux and choreography here echo certain scenes in Fellini's films, particularly the final scene of *Satyricon*, in which the patricians sit facing the camera, chewing away on the corpse of their wealthy friend.

***

A film with a fragmented narrative, such as *Andrei Rublev*, suggests, perhaps even demands, a fragmented essay.

***

The film is also a homage to horses. Horses gallop everywhere through it, much like the automobile would be ubiquitous in a fifties film about New York City. The Tatars, shown invading Russia at that time, ride extremely lively horses throughout, some kicking out their back legs in exuberance as they gallop about the town they have attacked. Near the beginning, Tarkovsky shows a horse rolling about on its back in seeming delight; another scene (in The Raid section) depicts a horse trying to negotiate its way down a flight of outdoor steps and falling over the side railing, landing upside down. The horse is immediately speared in the breast by a Tatar soldier, to put it out of its misery.

***

The film is filled with striking images, some of them horrific, some humorous: a cow rushes madly about inside a peasant woman's house, its back in flames; a jester flips upside down into a handstand, pulls down his pants and reveals a face painted on his bare ass; an artisan has his eyes gouged out; another man is tortured by Tatars by having red-hot metal from a melted down crucifix poured down his throat. Later, cool relief is provided the viewer by the camera dwelling on an extended close-up of the wind tossing leaves on a tree.

***

Rain, like milk, is another image repeated in many Tarkovsky films. The short final scene of *Andrei Rublev* – a frieze of four horses on an island in the medium distance standing in the rain – is one of the most beautiful in film. The horses are calm, flicking their tails or nodding their heads. Thus, this film, about art and artists, ends on a note of transcendent beauty.

4. 'The Bell' Chapter of *Andrei Rublev*

In the eighth and final chapter of Tarkovsky's *Andrei Rublev*, 'The Bell (1423-1424)', we are introduced to the character Boriska, the son of a master bell maker. Boriska's father has recently died of the plague. When the Prince's men come to the village looking for the bell maker, young Boriska tells them he is dead and convinces them that his father gave him the secret of bell making on his deathbed, though this is a lie. Normally, Boriska would help his father but he was no master bell maker.

Boriska is allowed to begin work on the project and puts all his youthful energy into it, working himself into a frenzy that saps his strength. Everything depends on the bell. The Prince, who has provided silver and copper for the bell, has made it clear that if Boriska fails and the bell cannot ring, then the young bell maker faces beheading. The bell is Boriska's great creative project, he bets everything on his ability to remember exactly how his father made bells. At the same time, he must trust his own creative ability. The bell is also *Andrei Rublev*, Tarkovsky's film itself. In the end, Boriska succeeds, the bell rings out over the countryside, Tarkovsky's film is complete. Andrei Rublev, the icon painter, finds the young man lying exhausted in a field; he holds him in his arms in a scene reminiscent of the Pieta. Boriska weeps, he is spent, utterly emptied from his great effort and the pressure and stress of completing the bell. Like making a film, making the bell involved an army of hands and helpers, as well as resolute, continuing effort and a trust in the creative. But Boriska is too fatigued to celebrate, he can only weep in the utter fatigue of his fulfillment.

The chapter ends with a long steady shot of burnt lumber, a tangle of blackened wood. Boriska, and Tarkovsky have burnt themselves to the core in order to accomplish their tasks, their great work.

The Epilogue that follows depicts a series of close-ups of Andrei Rublev's icon paintings, some resembling worn frescoes, others still vibrant with colour. The final icon reveals the face of Christ the Redeemer. As the camera slowly pans the image of Christ's face, the sound of distant thunder can be heard, accompanied by the refreshing, cleansing, fertile sound of a rainstorm. The icon fades into the image of the four horses standing on an island in the rain. We see the rain falling heavily, several of the horses swishing their tails. All is completed and fulfilled. All will be redeemed and renewed.

5. On the Spiritual in Film: Tarkovsky's *The Sacrifice*

Andrei Tarkovsky was arguably the most spiritual of filmmakers and *The Sacrifice* is, without a doubt, his most spiritual film.

A number of Tarkovsky quotations attest to the importance of the spiritual in his work (all quotes from Tarkovsky's book, *Sculpting in Time*):

"With man's help, the Creator comes to know himself."

"Art must transcend as well as observe; its role is to bring spiritual vision to bear on reality…"

"It is obvious to everyone that man's material aggrandisement has not been synchronous with spiritual progress."

"Artistic creation demands of the artist that he 'perish utterly'."

"Self-expression … is ultimately an act of sacrifice."

"The aim of art is to prepare a person for death, to plough and harrow his soul, rendering it capable of turning to good."

"In the end everything can be reduced to one simple element which is all a person can count upon in his existence: the capacity to love."

"… in the final analysis, the artistic image is always a miracle."

And finally, this startling quote that sounds as distinct and puzzling as a Zen koan: "Not knowing is noble, knowing is vulgar."

Despite his lifelong interest in icons and the Russian Orthodox Church, I suspect, by the tenor of the quotes above and from his films themselves, that Tarkovsky's interest in the spiritual had little to do with formal religion. Especially in *The Sacrifice*, he appears to be addressing or conjuring a spirituality that was alive in human beings long before Christianity or Islam or Judaism or the Greek and Roman gods, or Buddhism or Hinduism or even animist religions. His idea of the spiritual was something inherent in the individual human being, a longing to go beyond the self, a longing for sacrifice. Of course, this spirit can manifest under the banner of any religion but any particular religion is not its ultimate source for its source can only be the individual human heart.

In *The Sacrifice*, the paterfamilias, Alexander, discovers that he can only save the world, and his child and his family from nuclear annihilation by sacrificing himself. This sacrifice turns out to be more psychological than physical. He needs to break down completely his idea of who he is; he needs to 'perish utterly' in Tarkovsky's words. The vehicle that delivers this breakdown is a 'white' witch, a woman servant in his house. He must have sexual relations with her in order to alter fate. But this act destroys all his masks, all his beliefs about who he thinks he is. In the end, he watches as his house, consumed in flames, comes crashing down.

While Tarkovsky claimed he did not employ symbols in his films (when asked about symbols, he stated that "rain is rain...the Zone is a zone"), the burning house clearly represents the end of Alexander's world: his relationship with his family, his former life, all that he holds dear, his personality, all that he stands for, even his own mind. In the end, he is driven off in an ambulance, presumably to an asylum. For, in our times, it is considered pure madness to sacrifice oneself for the benefit of the world.

Tarkovsky wrote, expressing the ultimate dignity portrayed in *The Sacrifice*: "...love yourself so much that you respect in yourself the supra-personal, divine principal, which forbids you to pursue your acquisitive, selfish interests and tells you to give yourself, without reasoning or talking about it, to love others. This requires a true sense of your own dignity: an acceptance of the objective value and significance of the 'I' at the centre of your life on earth, as it grows in spiritual stature, advancing towards the perfection in which there can be no egocentricity."

6. Memorable Scenes from *Ivan's Childhood* by Andrei Tarkovsky

The opening shot: a beautiful blond-haired boy, Ivan, stands by a tree, looking at the viewer through the greenery. The camera slowly pans up the tree to the very top and gives us a view of the boy walking away.

***

Later, we are offered a view into a small stove, its fire raging. In the background, we hear the sound of trickling water.

***

Two beautiful children, Ivan and a young girl, sit on a truck loaded with apples. It's raining and the camera closes in on their rain-soaked faces. The apples are slick with rain as Ivan chooses one and hands it to her. Later, some of the apples will spill across a beach where several horses come to eat them. (Rain is another visual trope in Tarkovsky's films, the rain that is life-giving and fecund, and the rain that washes away and erases memory and the past.)

***

A warplane projects at a strange angle out of the earth where it crashed.

***

A serene close-up of a man's hand carefully placing two eggs, some chunks of dark bread, a piece of cheese on a cloth.

***

A beautiful young woman, a nurse, with dark hair and ivory skin stands in a forest thick with straight white birch trees.

***

The sky reflected in a swamp; distant flares falling from the heavens at night.

***

A strange metallic cross, with several circles at its centre, stands crookedly against the sky.

***

This film seems to represent and commemorate the murdered childhoods of millions of children during World War II, including the lost childhood of Tarkovsky himself, who nevertheless managed to survive the war itself.

7. On Andrei Tarkovsky's Film, *Nostalghia*

This is film as the art of contemplation. Tarkovsky, here as in his other films (especially *The Mirror*), employs long, lingering shots that ultimately suggest that the story isn't created there on the screen but in the viewer's imagination. For most modern viewers seeking fast-paced entertainment, Tarkovsky's approach could be maddening, eliciting a painful feeling of boredom. But for a viewer who can settle in and is willing to spend the time required, without recourse to speed and flash, a Tarkovsky film can be thoroughly enlightening and entertaining. *Nostalghia* is just such a film. When it first came out, the New York Times reviewer, Vincent Canby, said that this is a film in which "nothing happens". It's true – nothing happens, and it's marvellous.

Though the plot is fairly straightforward, the approach is not. Russian poet, Andrei Gorchakov, is in Italy to research the life of an 18th century Russian composer who had lived in Tuscany. Andrei employs a beautiful Italian translator, Eugenia, who falls in love with him and ends up leaving because the poet rebuffs her advances. Before this, they travel to an Italian village to view frescoes by Piero della Francesca in a Tuscan convent where the Madonna of Childhood is visited by young women hopeful for a child. In the village, Andrei meets Domenico, a rather mad prophet, who asks the poet to fulfill the odd task of carrying a lit candle across a mineral pool to save the world. Throughout, time is used by Tarkovsky as a tool of free association – scenes don't necessarily follow in a linear order.

Every frame in the film is a painting by Caravaggio or Rembrandt or Titian. If Caravaggio were a filmmaker, this is the film he would shoot. In one of those long takes that Tarkovsky loves, we see two bottles standing in the rain, slowly filling with rainwater as the two main characters walk about, talking. As in many of his films, the rain is falling indoors, in an old rundown house in the Italian countryside where Domenico lives. Although Tarkovsky would likely deny it ('rain is rain,' he said), for me this recurring image of indoor rain suggests the fecundity of imagination, the richness of inner worlds and dreamscapes.

A film by Tarkovsky is much like a long poem, with its recurring images that resonate with each other in a kind of visual rhyming. (I'm reminded of the Odyssey's repeated epithets about the 'wine-dark sea' and the 'rosy-fingered dawn'.) In *Nostalghia*, these images include mirrors (that often reflect the two main characters), circles, rain (as already mentioned), a dog, a child, mist, a ruin of a church open to the sky, lit candles. Even background sounds have their repetition: rain again, dripping water, clocks, ringing phones, voices, bells, and so on.

In some sense, everything is inverted in this world: rain falls indoors, roofless churches are open to the sky, out of nowhere a large dog suddenly appears in a hotel room.

The echo or resonance of several of these images and visual rhymes is subtle and intriguing. A round mirror in the hotel bathroom is later echoed by a bicycle wheel which is echoed by a high round empty window in the church ruin which is echoed by the rising sun. All these circles are roughly the same size on screen.

Many of the scenes in this film are stunning. In a chapel, a young woman kneels before the Madonna of Childbirth as she intones a prayer that reveals her longing for a child. At the end of the prayer, she pulls open the lower part of the Madonna's robes, suddenly releasing a dozen small birds on the air.

Tarkovsky is a master of scenes that incorporate his favourite images. In another scene, the police have rescued a family in the village after seven years of entrapment in their house by their father and husband, the mad Domenico, who fears the effect the craziness and absurdity of the world will have on his family. Once outside, the mother falls to her knees and kisses the earth. Right next to her, a full bottle of milk has fallen over and is chugging out its contents onto the ground. As noted earlier, milk appears as a significant image in every Tarkovsky film.

In another scene, Andrei takes an afternoon nap in his hotel room. We see him fully clothed, asleep on the bed. On one side of the room, the shutters have been opened wide and a heavy rain falls into thick foliage outside. On the other side, we see into a bathroom with the round mirror on the wall and a bentwood chair with a circle at its back. Suddenly, inexplicably, a large dog hurries out of the bathroom and settles on the floor next to the bed. There has been no indication that a dog was lurking in the bathroom. Is this the arrival of a dream? Perhaps. (Dogs can also symbolize madness, as in the 'black dogs' of depression.)

In another, later scene, mad Domenico has gone to Rome. We see him giving a speech about mankind's need to return to a simpler, less selfish way of life. The thin crowd appears to include escapees from an asylum. As he speaks, he stands on the hindquarters of the horse of Marcus Aurelius, a famous statue on the Piazza Campidoglio in the heart of Rome. At the end of his speech, he douses himself in gasoline and sets himself on fire, falling to the ground to the sound of a barking dog. Domenico, in flames, rolls to the feet of a person holding a sign which reads 'Tomorrow Is the End of the World'. The end of the world is, of course, another favourite Tarkovsky theme.

In the final scene of the film, we see Andrei, the Russian poet, and the dog sitting on the ground, a pool of water before them. Three thick, candle-shaped reflections can be seen in the pool. As the camera pulls back, we realize they are sitting inside the roofless church open to the sky. The reflections in the pool are from three tall empty windows high up in the church. We notice that everything is inside the church: the poet, the dog, the pool of water, a country house, the countryside. This being Tarkovsky with his interest in the spiritual life, the message here seems clear to me – not just the church and its contents are sacred but the entire world is sacred. Nothing is outside the church, nothing is outside the sacred realm. Nothing is excluded.

8. The Morphing of Fellini: Two Endings

In the final scenes of Fellini's *La Dolce Vita* (1960), the journalist, Marcello Rubini, (played by Marcello Mastroianni) has gone with a crowd of revellers to the beach near Rome to greet the dawn. His face shows the ravages of the all-night saturnalia he has attended. The scenes from the party clearly depicted the decadent lifestyle led by him and his companions. Now, as they walk along the seaside in first light, Marcello glimpses across an estuary a young girl with her family, a girl he had met earlier in another context. The beautiful girl is the absolute image of innocence and purity. He calls to her across the intervening water. She recognizes him. She puts her hand up to her ear. She can't hear because of the roaring of wind and the waves pounding the shore. She calls to him. He can't hear her either. Eventually, faced with the impossibility of communicating with this figure of innocence, he shrugs his shoulders, gives up and rejoins his dissolute friends.

In the final scene of Fellini's later major film, *Fellini Satyricon* (1969), Encolpio, the main character, who has been exploring the degraded and dissolute world that was imperial Rome, is heading to the seashore with a young friend. They hope to catch a sailing ship, whose masts and rigging can be glimpsed projecting above the sand dunes, and thence travel away to new worlds hopefully untouched by the decadence, depravity, and corruption of Rome. They long to begin life anew. As they walk, they pass a number of older patrician men sitting in rows on the benches of a small outdoor amphitheatre. All these men are staring straight ahead at the camera and chewing, chewing,

chewing. The looks on their faces appear blank and debauched. They are consuming the corpse of their colleague who has died. He was a powerful landowner whose will stipulated that his associates could only inherit his holdings if they actually consumed his flesh after his death. So, in their hunger for wealth, they are willing to debase themselves entirely by imitating cannibals. Meanwhile, we see the pair of young friends walking past, one of them dancing and gambolling about, and shouting, 'Vita! Vita! Vita!'.

The difference in the endings of these two films seems to signal a significant change in Fellini's view of the world. In both films, he explores decadence: first in modern Rome, then in ancient Rome. Both films end at the seashore. However, *La Dolce Vita* (the irony of the title is worth noting) appears to conclude with a clearly negative, perhaps even nihilistic, image – his character's inability to communicate with the world of innocence and life. The journalist shrugs his shoulders and gives up, his voice swallowed in the turbulence of wind and wave, as he is separated from the young innocent girl by the intervening estuary. He is lost in the tumult of life. On the other hand, in *Fellini Satyricon*, although he has again explored debauchery and decadence to the full, even depicting the cannibalism of the patricians, Fellini ends with a life-affirming shout to the heavens.

In the final shot of *Fellini Satyricon*, one of the most beautiful conclusions in film, the little sailing vessel and the two young characters morph into still images of an ancient fresco on a wall. The message is clear yet subtle: these two vital young men escaped, sailing away into a world more innocent and humane, full of promise and possibility. A world full of life.

ALIVE

In the midst of intense pain, a strange thought came to me. I was writhing on the bathroom floor at home in great agony with what would later prove to be an attack of acute appendicitis. But, in the meantime, I had to wait for a ride to the hospital.

As I lay there on the floor, there was nothing I could do to allay the pain, nothing I could take that would stay in my stomach. It was sharp and continuous and definitely the worst pain I had experienced in my life. This was the fourth time (and it would be the last) that an attack of this sort would visit me. The two previous years had brought three previous appendix attacks, not quite this intense. Each time I experienced one of these attacks, the doctors at the hospital emergency ward would tell me that they didn't think it was appendicitis. After a few hours, the pain would pass and they would send me home.

This time, the pain went on and on. Eventually, they would open me up to explore, find the offending appendix, and excise it. I would be cured.

But in the meantime, I'm writhing on the bathroom floor. In the midst of extreme pain, this is the unexpected thought that comes to me: "This is the worst pain I've ever experienced and yet I have never in my life felt so alive, so deeply alive."

I see this experience as the intensely personal equivalent of the social paradise that Rebecca Solnit writes about in *A Paradise Built in Hell*, in which she explores the extraordinary communities that arise in disaster. She writes: "We don't even have a language for this emotion, in which the wonderful comes wrapped in the terrible, joy in sorrow, courage in fear."

NOAH'S ARK AS LIBRARY

Noah's Ark was actually a library. It wasn't saving actual animals but preserving the names of animals, their descriptions, how they cantered or flew, how they mated and fought.

The Ark was saving language itself, its duality reflected in the pairing of the beasts and in the dualities inherent in language. In this sense, every library is an Ark, and every book too.

THE GLOBAL BIBLE

Today the Internet is the equivalent of the Bible – every argument one wishes to make, and its opposite, can be proven by some statement from an 'expert' on the Internet.

THE MATHEMATICS OF NOW

How long is the present moment? Is it $1/32^{nd}$ of a second, as has been stated? No, because within that space of time is a shorter 'now' lasting $1/64^{th}$ of a second; and within that is a shorter present moment lasting $1/128^{th}$ of a second; and within that a moment of 'now' lasting $1/256^{th}$ of a second. The present moment cannot be pinned down, it can only be experienced in its passing.

PSYCHIC BIRTHPLACES

From the novel, *Monsieur* by Lawrence Durrell (the first book in his Avignon quartet): "...the Chinese fancy that one has two birthplaces – one the real physical one, and one which is a place of predilection, the place in which one was psychically born."

I think that psychic birthplaces, unlike the physical one, can be multiple. Psychic birthplaces are those locations where we have a sudden insight or connection to our future or the depth of our being, to what is drawing us toward our fate.

As far as I can recall, the location of my first psychic birthplace was a corner store in Toronto owned by a relative of my mother's. I was about eight years old and had been feasting all day with my little cousins on free candy from the store. My mother's cousin, whom I called 'aunt,' had said, "*Take as much as you want*," and we did, stuffing our little gobs without control.

At the height of our childish gorging, a knife-sharpener, pushing his plain cart with its stone wheel, passed by the door looking for business. Our eyes met. He was obviously poor and I thought he looked profoundly sad. Even though I was just a child, for some reason my heart opened to him. Maybe, on some level, the contrast between my childish indulgence and his poverty and need touched me. I learned in that moment the taste of deep compassion (and maybe a little about guilt too). It wasn't pity I felt, but the profound sense of the common humanity we shared. I believe I felt what he felt.

Psychic birthplaces can be multiple, happening over and over again. At Delphi in Greece, I stood on the top of the mountain, alone by the gaming field, among the ancient Delphic ruins. I was a nineteen-year-old college student traveling through Europe. At that moment, I felt a charged presence that woke me to the rich possibilities inherent in our world. An invisible presence that was intelligent and all-seeing was apparent to me. It had nothing to do with ghosts, but I felt the ever-present awareness, the force of life, that moves through the world.

Years later, I visited a community centre in Ottawa. There I was being told by a lovely young woman, the director of the centre, that she could not give me a job to teach poetry, a job I badly needed for the meagre pay it offered. But it didn't matter. Something else was going on. I felt an incredibly strong connection to this woman. Months later, by lucky coincidence we were introduced in a grocery store by a common friend. We connected, and eventually married. (We're still married.)

During a three-month meditation retreat at an old hotel in central Pennsylvania, I was in the bedroom of my Buddhist teacher, Chogyam Trungpa Rinpoche. I had been ushered in to present him his morning tea offering. Kneeling by the side of the bed where he sat, I held up the tray with two bowls – one filled with dry gunpowder tea, the other with hot water. As he sat on the side of the bed and looked at me, his eyes appeared to be all pupil. When he lifted a few grains of tea to drop into the hot water, it suddenly sounded like boulders rolling down a mountain. My awareness of the world expanded immensely. It was a glimpse of how spacious and rich the universe could be when one actually let go into the unconditional. It lasted but a moment but, in another sense, it never left.

And finally, years later, following the birth of my son, I fell to weeping with joy and relief as I stood in the shower. I was racked with sobs of the most intense emotion I've ever experienced. Years after that, I heard my wife weeping with similar intensity in the shower following the death of her father. Perhaps my final psychic birthplace will be the location of my own death.

Beehive

All the senses, excepting touch, are focused mainly in the head, that beehive with seven holes that sits on the shoulders, a fever-box of frenetic activity.

The eyes, like a pair of queen bees, watch over the fields, translating colours, shapes, directions. The expanse of their clear focus is approximately ninety degrees, with an additional ninety degrees or so of clouded images as seen from the corners of the eyes.

As for the sense of taste, in conjunction with smell (perhaps they are actually two aspects of a single sense), the focus can be subtly panoramic. We taste what we smell and we smell what we taste. The panoramic aspect is especially true of smell, for one can taste what touches the tongue but the scent of frying garlic drifts out the door of the kitchen and into the neighbour's yard, and that of a forest fire or pulp mill travels for miles.

The hearing sense is also panoramic, a full 360 degrees – one can hear a plate dropped behind one without seeing it, the crows behind me are just as noisy as those in front. Sounds fill a space completely.

Touch is arguably the sense of which we are least conscious, especially in our human world, which focuses on colour for the eyes, music for the ears, sugar and salt for the tongue, garbage and perfume for the nose. The feel of surfaces incorporates a wide range of subtle difference. When was the last time you compared the feel of objects on the tips of the fingers: the smoothness of paper, the distinctly different smoothness of the plastic cellphone, the wood of the desk, the complex ripple of hair, the cool glass of the watch face, the watch's knobby leather strap? Cotton, silk, satin all feel different, and differ again from wool, rayon and nylon. The feel of oil, water, snow, and ice. The subtle but inescapable distinctions between iron and aluminum. And touch, of course, is not limited to the fingers: the softness of the rug under bare feet, the feel of sand, of hot tarmac. The feel of clothes on the back, of wind in the face, of cold or heat on skin.

Short Essays on Poetry

1. Falling Through the Poem

On entering a poem, you should feel as if you have leapt from a high cliff. We would think, as we are falling through the poem, through space, that the last line should feel like hitting the ground, but what if the last line is realizing that there is no ground? In fact, the last line should feel as if the earth has opened up beneath you.

2. Commentary on Basho's Most Famous Haiku

The literal translation is as follows:

> Old pond   *Furuike ya*
> Frog jumping into   *Kawazu tobikomu*
> Water sound   *Mizu no oto*

This is not a new pond but an old one. A new pond would suggest the nearby sound of trickling water whereas an old pond suggests calmness, silence. It's been there forever, reflecting the sky.

The frog is simply 'frog', with no modifiers – not old or new, not green or plump. That single unadorned word suggests stillness; not a frog with its tongue flicking out, but one that waits.

Then comes the shock of sudden movement. He's jumping. What is he jumping into? The pond, of course. But look closely – the words say he is jumping, not only into the pond, but 'into the sound', as if the sound were already there, pre-existent, waiting for him as he was waiting.

Basho was a Buddhist, and likely held a Buddhist view of time. Everything already exists in this moment. Everything that has ever happened, everything that will ever happen, is happening in this moment. Nothing can happen outside this moment. At the moment the frog is jumping into the pond he is also jumping into the 'water sound'. One doesn't really follow the other. The moment is simply the process of future becoming past. The future doesn't really exist; it hasn't arrived yet. The past doesn't exist either. It's gone. Shockingly, the present also doesn't exist. It's simply that process of future becoming past with no way to fix the moment.

The pond is 'old', the past. The splash is the unknown future. They come together in the frog's stillness and the frog's motion. The three lines of Basho's haiku contain everything, and nothing.

3. Poetry, Music, and Dylan's Nobel Prize

The Nobel Committee should seriously consider offering a prize for music separate from the prize for literature. While I believe Bob Dylan's work was certainly deserving of the award (conferred in 2016), it seems that a prize for music would have been more appropriate.

As I revisit certain lyrics from the Dylan songbook, it strikes me that there are many lines that work in a song that just don't work on the page. This has everything to do with the heavy, straight-up rhymes, which always clunk on the inner ear when read and yet add marvellously to the music when sung.

In the song, *Idiot Wind*, "Idiot Wind, blowing every time you move your mouth / Blowing down the backroads headin' south", the obvious rhymes of *mouth/south* sound just fine when sung, but when read on the page prove painful on the inner ear. These conventional rhymes appear in many songs, such as *Visions of Johanna (soft/off)*, *Every Grain of Sand (sea/me)*; *Brownsville Girl (burn/learn)*. In the end, they sound rather juvenile to the inner ear, like something out of a child's book of poems. But, once again, they all work well when sung.

However, what is known as slant rhyme (also called oblique rhyme), is a much more subtle and intriguing sound device. When Dylan's songs employ slant rhymes, they sound far better to the mind's ear when read on the page. Again, from *Idiot Wind (teeth/ breathe), Visions of Johanna (entwined/mind)*; Every Grain of *Sand (man/sand)*; and, especially, this slant rhyme from *Gates of Eden (sun/Eden)*. Even a few of these slant rhymes can sound heavy on the ear when read but they are certainly an improvement on *mouth/south*.

If the Nobel Committee ever did accede to a Nobel Prize for Music, they could then give the award to Yo Yo Ma, Arvo Paart, Leonard Cohen (if he were still with us), Joni Mitchell, and whatever Beatles remain alive. At that point the discussion and argument concerning literary merit of musical lyrics would disappear.

4. The Poem Writes Itself

One theory of the Paleolithic cave paintings, that comes from certain indigenous beliefs, is that the paintings painted themselves – they simply appeared one day on the cave walls.

An extension of this theory leads to the speculation that all art creates itself: the paintings paint themselves, stories tell themselves, poems write themselves. Look at it this way – the poet gathers all the requirements for the poem: he has studied the history of poetics, he readies paper and pen, the tiny worm of inspiration begins to glow in his head. At that point, he has set out all the fundamentals of the poem and the poem begins to write itself, the worm begins to crawl forth.

Looked at in another way, there exists an underground river of the creative that is always there – the artist, the poet, the musician dips his pen, his brush, his flute into this flow and the creative breaks to the surface. The artist has done nothing but prepare all the necessary conditions and open to the possibilities. The poet then dips his pen and the poem writes itself.

5. On the Poem

"... man ... the one who produces symbolic forms, systems of signs, and who then confuses them with 'reality' itself ..."
—René Girard, *Things Hidden Since the Foundation of the World*

Just as the 'word' is not the 'thing', so the explication of the poem is not the poem. The poem must stand on its own, ineffable. In the same way, the explanation or understanding of reality is not the experience of reality itself.

6: Haiku and Meditation

Every moment of life is utterly unique. That is what haiku tries to reveal, to unveil, without recourse to anything outside its own words and images – no greater meaning, no philosophy.

That's why meditation is simply an 'expression' of enlightenment (not a struggle to the peak of the mountain), an expression of each unique moment, an expression of being awake – not based on some rule, technique, philosophy, or goal – simply based on the experience of that unique moment of life, and the next one, and the next.

FOREVER INTO NEVERLAND

A quote from a 1922 silhouette film on Cinderella by Lotte Reiniger (viewed in an exhibition at MOMA): "She curtsies and passes forever into neverland."

What intrigues me about this quote is that combination of 'forever' and 'neverland' – as if it references the eternity of nothingness, which is the only thing that can be eternal, for anything that is existent is subject to change, impermanence, and dissolution, and will ultimately pass from one state to another. Only nothingness is eternal and unchanging.

Monotheism: A Speculative Essay

Thousands of years ago, something in human culture sparked the move from animism and pantheism to monotheism. What was it exactly?

Freud wrote in *Moses and Monotheism*, his final book, that monotheism came, in fact, from the Egyptians and not from the early days of Judaism, as many believed at the time. Yet there appear to be even earlier possible antecedents for monotheism. Certain sects of Hinduism in Vedic India could be called monotheistic, and the Zoroastrians of ancient Persia also held monotheistic beliefs. The actual roots of monotheism can be traced as far as back as the early Iron Age.

Eventually, in an irreversible move to the west (ideas, like goods such as silk and spices, always seemed to move east to west along the trade routes), monotheism became a prime feature of Judaism. From there it was clearly passed on to Christian and Islamic worlds, eventually replacing the pantheistic religions of Greece and Rome. What prompted this acceptance of monotheism as a replacement for pantheism across a large portion of the European, Middle Eastern, and North African worlds?

According to Freud, it was a collective neurosis termed 'longing for the father'. Why Freud considered that this longing was a neurosis is best left for another discussion. In any case, monotheism itself was far from monolithic. Within monotheism, there exists a range of beliefs. While Islam is apparently strictly monotheistic, Christianity preaches a tri-partite monotheism: God the Father, God the Son, and God the Holy Ghost.

This concept of a tri-partite God could easily have been adapted from the much earlier Hindu belief in three main gods: Brahma, Vishnu, and Shiva. I cannot help but ask: Could the inclusion of a 'divine' human (Jesus Christ) be a subtle influence and adaptation from non-theistic Buddhism, in which the Buddha is considered simply a highly evolved human being, but not divine? Obviously, the flow of information and religious philosophy moved quite readily across the Eurasian landmass. As proof of this cross-fertilization stretching from the far Far East to Europe, Jared Diamond in *Guns, Germs, and Steel* points out that many of the same plants and animals were domesticated across this region. This exchange of information and ideas goes back well into pre-history. The Buddhist view could easily have passed along those same routes.

Many other forms of early monotheism offered slight variations. Even some animist religions could be called slightly monotheistic, and of course, the Greeks, while pantheistic, held that Zeus was the head of the gods. In any case, Wilhelm Schmidt's theory of primitive monotheism, or ur-monotheism, that is, a monotheism that existed prior to pantheism, has been widely debunked by more recent theories.

It is also intriguing to note that various types of monotheism posit various types of Godhead. Some resemble energies or powers or divine will, and others lean more to a personification in imitation of human beings, the father in particular. Sometimes the Godhead was a great warrior or creator of the cosmos, and, for most of these believers, He was always the True God and all other gods were fabrications. In ancient China, he was called Heaven (Shangdi), an omnipotent force, with his earthly manifestation in the form of the emperor. In all of these contexts, Godhead is almost always considered of masculine gender.

Perhaps Freud was on to something, as the growth of agriculture seemed also to lead to a growing patriarchy in the family structure. Was this then reflected in a monotheistic religious belief? Or was the end of pantheism and the appearance of monotheism influenced by the growth of cities, with the centralization of power suggesting a monotheistic world-view? Or was there something in pantheism that was failing human beings and required the corrective of monotheism? Or was there something in the evolution of the written word, with its power and control placed in a literate priesthood, which prompted monotheism? Or was it all of these together?

It is also intriguing to note that monotheism appears to prompt a view that there is, not only one supreme deity, but also only one official, authoritative text, a singular 'scripture'. One God, One Book: The Torah for the Jews, the Bible for the Christians, the Koran for the Muslims.

And what will come after monotheism? Is the breakdown of the family, the growth of matriarchal power around the world, the diminution of power among priesthoods and elites going to lead to the fading of monotheism and the birth of something new? These devolutions and evolutions move at a continent-shifting pace but something is surely changing in this aspect of the human story.

Despair/Serenity

The overwhelming vastness of the landscape in a traditional Chinese painting (in which man is a mere stroke in that landscape), can prompt a certain despair. The same can be said when contemplating the infinite latitude-less reaches of the night sky. For some, despair can arise when one realizes how infinitesimal and unimportant one's own life can appear in the overall scheme of time and space.

On the other hand, that realization of infinite vastness, within and without, can give rise to a profound sense of serenity. In the immensity of the universe, all my problems, all my accomplishments and dreams, all my worries, hopes and fears are the merest dust falling forever through space.

The English Written Word as a Medium for Poetry

I. The Poetry of Etymology

Ernest Fenollosa's *The Chinese Written Character as a Medium for Poetry* was written in 1903. Later edited by Ezra Pound and published in 1918, ten years after Fenollosa's death, this short essay proved a seminal document in the history of 20th century Anglo-American poetics, influencing everyone from Pound himself to William Butler Yeats and T.S. Eliot. Fenollosa opened the gates to a flood of Japanese and Chinese poetry in translation throughout the century from dozens of poets including Kenneth Rexroth and W.S. Merwin. While some scholars of China and Japan consider Fenollosa's work seriously flawed, there remains no doubt that Fenollosa influenced the mainstream of Modernist poetry in the English-speaking world.

In the essay, Fenollosa wrote, "In this (*calligraphy*) the Chinese symbol shows its advantage. Its etymology is constantly visible. It retains the creative impulse and process, visible and at work. ... The very soil of Chinese life seems entangled in the roots of its speech. The manifold illustrations which crowd its annals... all these are flashed at once on the mind as reinforcing values with an accumulation of meaning which a phonetic language can hardly hope to attain." *(Italics added.)*

Let me begin by pointing out that the typical native Chinese speaker of Mandarin or Cantonese is apparently no more aware of 'the accumulation of meaning' or 'the roots of its speech' that are found in Chinese written characters than native speakers of English are aware of the etymologies (root histories) of words in their own language.

Though Fenollosa is correct in stating that the possibilities of metaphor and poetry are apparent *visually* in the Chinese written character, the native Chinese speaker is not only hardly cognizant of these possibilities but, in fact, shows little interest in them. Because language is an ever present, everyday practical tool, so common as to be nearly invisible, its subtler nuances, meanings, and histories tend to be ignored, except by those with a distinct interest in linguistics, poetry, or other forms of writing. The poetry that is apparent in the complex construction of written characters, in the layering of Chinese ideograms, generally goes unnoticed and unremarked.

At the same time, English etymology is as rich and deep in metaphoric and poetic possibilities as Chinese, with this significant difference – the connections among English roots and cognates are not visual (as they are, of course, in Chinese written characters) and are often extremely subtle as well as hidden from the average English speaker (and reader).

The poetry, and the possibilities for metaphor, in English etymology are found in the intriguing relations between and among words and their cognates and roots.

While English does not provide anything as obvious as the Chinese character for 'see' – a stylized 'eye' above a modified picture of running legs and one of Fenollosa's first examples in his essay – fascinating poetic connections are clearly apparent between and among many English words.

To take one example (all examples are from *Origins* by Eric Partridge) – the word 'verse' is in the same family as the words 'towards', 'forwards', 'backward'; the '-ward' element connecting to a root word that means 'a turning'. The Indo-European (IE) root is 'wert' or 'wart' (Sanskrit), 'to turn'. Other cognates in this family include: versatile, version, vertical, vertebrate, vortex, universe, and weird.

Also related is the Russian 'versta', that is a line or row, and Middle Latin 'versus', a furrow. This connection, between a furrow and a verse is certainly one rich with poetic, visual and metaphoric possibilities. A line of furrows in a ploughed field can be seen to resemble a page of verse and reminds this reader that the Greek writing known as 'boustrophedon' (or 'ox-writing' from the Greek 'bous', ox) refers to writing based on the way an ox ploughs a field – left to right, then back again right to left, then back again left to right, and so on.

A simpler example of the poetry and suggestiveness inherent in etymology is found in the word 'sane' which finds its root in the Sanskrit 'isanyati', he progresses, with cognates including sanitary, from the Latin 'sanitus' or learned, and the Late Latin, 'sanitas', a healing. It doesn't take too sharp an imagination to see the poetic connections among such words as sanity, progress, learning, and healing.

The history of words is replete with arcane knowledge of all sorts. A brush, from the Sanskrit for 'point', is connected to the word 'brushwood' with the understanding that, as Eric Partridge states, the first brushes were likely not made of animal bristles but of stems and twigs.

Sometimes the etymological connections prove bizarre. Take the word 'fornicate', which comes from the Latin 'fornix', an arc, an arched vault, hence an underground brothel, with connections to the Latin words for oven and furnace.

In another example, the word 'medical' has an intriguing connection to the Indo-European root, 'me-', to measure and is cognate with remedy and meditation.

In Shakespeare's *Henry VI, Part I*, the character Bedford says:
> *Comets, importing change of times and states,*
> *Brandish your crystal tresses in the sky*

Shakespeare clearly makes use of the poetry inherent in word origins with his image of 'crystal tresses', as the English word 'comet' comes from the Greek, *kometes*, which means 'long-haired'.

And finally, in another example rich in poetic metaphor, the word 'mirror' can be traced back to the Late Latin, 'miraculum', a miracle, as well as the Latin, 'mirari', to wonder, and the Latin 'mirus', astonishing, strange, wonderful. Further, the Indo-European root for mirror, 'mei-' is connected to the word 'to laugh' and the Sanskrit, 'smayate', he smiles. The poetic possibilities that blossom from these relationships are nothing less than marvelous (another cognate in this family).

There is no doubt that one can find wonderful suggestions of poetry in the complexities of Chinese written characters. The language is fairly bursting with them once one starts looking. The same can be said of the English language and its etymologies.

II. "A True Noun Does Not Exist"

In the same essay, Fenollosa wrote, "A true noun, an isolated thing, does not exist in nature. Things are only the terminal points, or rather more precisely the meeting points of actions, cross-sections cut through actions, snap-shots. Neither can a pure verb, an abstract motion, be possible in nature. The eye sees noun and verb as one: things in motion, motion in things, and so the Chinese conception tends to represent them."

"The character for 'sun' underlying the sign for 'bursting forth of plants' = spring.

The 'sun' sign tangled in the branches of the 'tree sign' = east.

'Rice-field' plus 'struggle' = male.

'Boat' plus 'water' = a ripple."

Several paragraphs on, he adds, "The truth is that acts are successive, even continuous; one causes or passes into another. And though we may string never so many clauses into a single, compound sentence, motion leaks everywhere, like electricity from an exposed wire. All processes in nature are interrelated; and thus there could be no complete sentence (according to this definition) save one which it would take all time to pronounce."

And finally, in *Synopsis of Lectures on Chinese and Japanese Poetry* (1903), Fenollosa writes, "A noun is a cross section cut through an act."

In the early years of the twentieth century, Henri Poincaré, a French mathematician and physicist, said much the same: "The things themselves are not what science can reach..., but only the relations between things. Outside of these relations there is no knowable reality."

These comments taken together are a linguistic expression of the Buddhist concept of interdependence, which is the foundation argument for the idea of 'emptiness' in the highest teachings of Buddhist philosophy. (Fenollosa was a convert to Buddhism.) Emptiness, in this context, has little to do with the rather negative slant the word is given in English. From a Buddhist point of view, emptiness is simply openness, or the space that allows.

In order to consider how the idea of interdependence relates to emptiness, let us take an isolated noun which Fenollosa claimed does not exist in nature.

Consider a single sheet of paper. The sheet of paper does not exist in isolation. It exists in the realm of interdependence. Its existence is dependent on:

- The tree that was made into pulp to produce the paper.
- The existence of the tree depends on the seed from a previous tree and that tree depends on a seed from an earlier tree and so on back as far as one can go.
- The paper is dependent on the man who cut the tree down for pulp and that man's existence depends on the existence of his parents, grandparents, ancestors as far back as one can go.
- The paper also is dependent on the factory where it was made and those who built the factory all of whose

existence depended on parents, grandparents, ancestors and so on.

- The paper's existence here at this moment depends on the truck that brought it to the store, the oil and gas for the truck and all that those depend on, the truck driver and his interdependent existence and so on.
- The paper also depends on the existence of the store in which it was sold, the builders of that store, the people who fed the builders and grew their food and so on and on.

Thus it becomes clear that, like the noun 'paper', the existence of the sheet of paper in reality is utterly interdependent and therefore the paper has no independent existence outside this web of relationships. The noun too, as language, exists only in a web of etymological and root-word relations, its family of cognates.

Like the complete sentence which it would take "all time to pronounce", the existence of the sheet of paper depends on the entire rest of the world through all of time. And yet, here is the sheet of paper. It shimmers, luminous, before the eyes. It exists in its details. It can be seen by the eyes, touched, smelt. But it is changing every moment and it exists separate *from nothing and no one.*

The noun and the thing are both empty. Empty of independent existence and yet shimmering, luminous, ever-changing before the eyes in this very moment.

THE ARTIST DISAPPEARS

The greatest artists disappear into their art. That's why so many questions remain about the identities of Homer, Shakespeare, and the authors of the Bible, as well as the makers of the Pyramids, the Venus da Milo, and Macchu Picchu. In the East too, it is said that Lao Tzu, author of the Taoist classic, the *Tao Te Ching*, is likely a combination of several people. Quite simply, the art lives on while the artist disappears.

STORY

Is a story that can be told once only and heard once only still a story? Is story's essence repetition or the original creation, or the combination of the two?

Imagine a story that disappeared the moment after you revealed it, a story without past or future.

We are that too.

Unified Field Epiphany

It happened while I was walking on the treadmill in late afternoon: the scales fell from my eyes, the apple fell from the tree, the penny dropped, things fell into place (and other clichés) – it definitely had that effortless quality of falling. That morning I had completed my 34th of 38 radiation treatments for prostate cancer, so perhaps the great intelligent machine that bathed me daily in its invisible glow and emitted a sound like a mechanical cicada, had connected a few synapses that had never previously linked up (or maybe unlinked a few).

So, what happened, what was the epiphany that accompanied my treading the treadmill? I realized that many of the areas of interest that I had been following for the past thirty years were, unbeknownst to me until that moment, actually connected. Everything I had been working on suddenly synched up, became layered and synthesized (like the rippling skein or stack of colour samples in Marcel Duchamp's last oil painting, *Tu m'*, 1918 – that's the visual image that came to mind that afternoon).

What came together, or was synthesized, so to speak, was the following:

- Visual elements from the origins of the alphabet (Proto-Sinaitic), which still linger back there deep in our brains in a kind of subliminal echo of linguistic history when we read words made up of letters.
- Calligraphed Chinese characters and the poetic impact of their visual elements (with much influence from Ernest Fenollosa).
- The idea that form and content can resonate with each other in both poetry and prose, with its own synthesis and unifying

of the visual element, the sound element and the meaning element. (*See the earlier essay in this collection*, Orange Gardens and Bedsprings: A Theory of Language.)

1. The Alphabet

First, the alphabet. Most readers or speakers of English have no idea that the letters of our alphabet are based on Proto-Sinaitic images or hieroglyphs from about 1500 B.C. (As stated earlier in this collection, the Ugarites and Phoenicians also came up with their own alphabets around the same period but theirs were written in cuneiform.) In the Proto-Sinaitic version, the written letter A was based on the picture of an ox-head, B was a house, D was a fish, E was a calling or praying figure, K was the palm of the hand, M was water, S was a bow and so on. Although one might conclude that members of the priest caste invented the Proto-Sinaitic alphabet, strong arguments have been made that suggest the alphabet actually came from Canaanite labourers in Egypt who required a simplified version of Egyptian hieroglyphics for their work. In order to simplify written language, they must have chosen already existing pictographs to represent the letters of the alphabet and their sounds. The echo of those images exists somewhere as subliminal traces in our brains, memories of the original visual content of the alphabet.

The ultimate history of most of our letters is visual. (However, it should be noted that the Greek-sourced letters – X, Y, Z, etc. – came later and have no apparent concrete, visual ancestors in the Proto-Sinaitic.)

2. Chinese Characters

The second element in this unified epiphany comes from Fenollosa's work on Chinese characters and poetry. In re-reading Fenollosa's essays, I was reminded of what the filmmaker, Andrei Tarkovsky, said about shooting a film: "If the regular length of a shot is increased, one becomes bored, but if you keep on making it longer, it piques your interest, and if you make it even longer, a new quality emerges, a special intensity of attention." This is clearly an attempt to employ the natural inclination for contemplation in the art of film.

I've experienced the same with certain books that might be difficult or dry (or might have less interesting sections). I keep reading. I'm getting nothing out of it. It's rather boring. I keep reading further and something, a line, piques my interest. I keep reading further, letting the boredom be boredom, and as I keep reading a new quality emerges, a special 'intensity of attention'. Sparks start to go off in my brain. Beyond the boredom, ideas start to arise, new connections, and so on. It doesn't always happen, it doesn't always work. But this is what happened as I was reading *The Chinese Written Character as a Medium for Poetry* and *Synopsis of Lectures on Chinese and Japanese Poetry* by Fenollosa.

In the latter essay (less an essay than a compendium of thoughts and notes), Fenollosa writes concerning Chinese written characters: "The Synthesis of the metaphorical overtones among the related words. / This is a great poetical dimension that exists fully in no other language. / This synthetic, versus our analytic sentences. / Only synthetic thought is really Poetic." While I certainly cannot agree with Fenollosa that this 'poetical dimension' only exists in Chinese, the word that interests me here is 'synthesis'. A 'synthesis' is a complex whole formed by combining elements. For Fenollosa, it was the synthetic aspect of Chinese written characters that was of interest: the combining of visual ideograms to make a character presented real metaphorical and poetical possibilities for him. (Obviously, the word 'synthetic' has a negatively charged meaning in our day, referring to that which is 'not genuine'. That is definitely not the meaning being applied here.)

This bringing together of elements in language, this synthesis, Fenollosa relates to the ancient Chinese philosophy of Harmony. He writes: "We (in the West) sniff at figure as useless embroidery. / But it is really a higher and more synthetic kind of truth. / An approach to the infinity and simultaneity of Nature itself." For the Chinese, traditionally, harmony encompasses and 'harmonizes' the fundamental principles of nature, society and humanity. Fenollosa points out that the Chinese language creates an intimate connection between man and nature. He adds, "With us (*again, he means the West*) human struggle, horror, tragedy, effort, is the supreme subject of poetry. / With them it is harmony, on many a plane. / Thus landscape art was born so early in the East." (*Italics added.*)

3. Unified Field

This bringing together of disparate elements into a new whole, this synthesis of linguistic elements, forms the essence of Harmony.

This linguistic harmony appears in English as well as Chinese. When prose or poetry synthesizes meaning with sound and with the visual, the ultimate possibilities of language are attained. Here, as Fenollosa would put it, Language reflects Nature, contains all the possible elements required of a 'natural' language, complete and harmonious.

A curious and sometimes unsubtle version of this synthesis is concrete poetry. One of the first, and most successful of concrete poets, was Guillaume Apollinaire, especially in his collection of poems titled *Calligrammes*. To take just one example, the words of the poem, 'The Little Car', are arranged on the page in such a way that they represent a little automobile, including the wheels, two passengers, a driver and the steering wheel. Of course, this is somewhat obvious and heavy-handed, although it can be a delightful poetic game.

At its highest level, this approach of synthesizing the visual aspect of words with their meaning can be found in the overall tone and structure of many novels, where the pacing, imagery, flow of language, and so on all contribute to the greater whole. Thus, a novel that wishes to project sadness or grief might contain long, flowing lines with a surfeit of heavy, weighty words. Or a section of a novel that depicts a walk in the country might read with a lightness and ease that reflects the entire situation of the character's world and state of mind. In many cases this is so perfectly integrated into the tone of the work as to be almost unnoticeable. In some sense, it tends to arise naturally in the novelist's (or poet's) choice of words and style.

The samples that appear earlier in this book, from Beckett and Conrad for example (in the essay titled *Orange Gardens and Bedsprings*), are cases in which this synthesis of textual structure and meaning are understated and brilliant. Clearly, the examples from Becket and Conrad and others echo, in an extremely subtle way, Fenollosa's view on the Chinese written character as a medium for poetry.

This synthesis of meaning with other elements of language such as structure, etymological history, even the somewhat hidden images of the letters of the alphabet, makes for a unified field of language, one that brings all the aural and visual elements of language into play and thence into harmony.

ACKNOWLEDGEMENTS

I would like to thank a number of people (associates, friends and family), who provided helpful comments on these essays: Nicola Vulpe, Susan Robertson, Reynold F. Frutkin, Murray Wilson, John Negru and Vincenzo Pietropaolo. And, of course, my partner, Faith Seltzer. Thank you so much, all of you, for your assistance. (And, my apologies if I missed anyone.)

Several of these essays first appeared in *Arc Magazine: Falling Through the Poem, Commentary on Basho's Most Famous Haiku*, and *Haiku and Meditation*.

ABOUT THE AUTHOR

Mark Frutkin has published eighteen books, including fiction, nonfiction, poetry, and essays. The novel, *Fabrizio's Return* (Knopf Canada) won the Trillium Award for best book in Ontario, and the Sunburst Award, and was a finalist for the Commonwealth Book Prize. The novel, *Atmospheres Apollinaire* (Porcupine's Quill), was a finalist for the Governor General's Award for fiction and the Trillium Award. His novels and poetry collections have been shortlisted five times for the Ottawa Book Award. In addition to Canada, his books have been published in the US and Great Britain, and in translation in Quebec, Italy, Holland, Russia, Poland, South Korea, and Turkey. His most recent novel, *The Artist and the Assassin* (Porcupine's Quill), based on the life of famous Italian painter, Caravaggio, won the Silver Medal in the Literary Fiction category of the IPPY Awards for books from independent publishers in US, Canada and Australia.

Printed in April 2023
by Gauvin Press,
Gatineau, Québec